THE 1% RULE

HOW TO FALL IN LOVE WITH THE PROCESS AND ACHIEVE YOUR WILDEST DREAMS

TOMMY BAKER

ISBN-13: 978-1-9856-3548-7

ISBN-10: 1985635488

Dedication

For Taylor – you inspire me daily and support me in everything I set out to create.

Get Inspired and Live the Life of Your Dreams!

Are you ready to get inspired? Join us each week for riveting conversations that extract the knowledge, inspiration, and practical action steps needed to live the life of your dreams! Our top-rated podcast and coaching platform, Resist Average Academy, will bring you this, and more!

Subscribe now on iTunes or listen online through Stitcher, Spotify, or Google Play and www.ResistAverageAcademy.com.

CONTENTS

INTRODUCTION

Our current system *isn't* working.

Specifically, our system for setting goals and staying motivated enough to not only see them to completion, but consistently break through new levels of achievement and fulfillment.

Over the course of the last half decade, I've immersed myself in answering a few basic questions and have gone down the rabbit hole to explore these answers.

These questions are simple, yet incredibly complex at the same time.

They include:

Why do some people achieve massive success in everything they do, *while others can't get out of their own way?*

What separates those who get excited and inspired for a season, a quarter, a month or a week, *and those who are consistently on fire?*

What are the core principles, mindsets, habits, and rituals of those who execute ruthlessly, ***and those who sit on the sidelines pondering?***

This led me on a personal quest of self-discovery and growth as I traveled the world to learn from the best. It led me to invest hundreds of thousands of dollars in seminars, programs, courses, and mentors. It led me to launching my own content platform, podcast, and coaching and consulting business, and to writing my first book and leading my own intensive experiences.

Nothing was off limits. Instead of pursuing the answers to these questions in one context, I attacked them from all angles. Sometimes, it'd be in the realm of physical health and pushing my body to its limits. Another time it would be a deep spiritual retreat or a transformational experience. Many would be in the context of entrepreneurship and the principles of wealth production.

My thirst for this knowledge was unquenchable.

During this time, I started to uncover the answers to the questions I'd asked for so long. I also started to connect the dots between *seemingly* unrelated contexts. It all finally started to make sense.

Most importantly, I started to experience this shift in my

own life, letting go of the old patterns of thinking and doing I'd created in order to step into new realities and experiences.

This led me to a powerful realization:

Nothing separates you and me from those whom we admire and look up to at the top of the mountain—we're one and the same.

The only difference is the way they define and perceive success, their level of clarity around goal setting, and their associated behaviors and habits. I also realized there were crucial yet common myths we had to let go of in order to step into a place of powerful execution. Once we were able to adopt these new patterns, we too would become unstoppable.

These insights and realizations, discovered through a decade-long journey of both research and experiential training, led to the creation of the book you're reading now.

My first book, *UnResolution*, was about dropping the mindset of waiting to achieve our goals, specifically the New Year's myth. This new book is about a *lifelong* mindset that allows for incredible achievement and a deep-rooted fulfillment pertaining to the basic human desire of wanting to be *better* today than yesterday.

The 1% Rule was born from watching so many great people with amazing intentions never move the needle long enough to produce results. Ultimately, they would give up on their dreams, go back to their corporate offices, retreat on their health goals, disengage in their relationships, and cease all momentum.

Their dreams would become a distant memory as time passed. They'd stay stuck for years on end, feeling worse as each birthday passed until they ultimately gave up and decided they were destined to stay the same.

If this sounds familiar, don't fret. No matter how out of touch you feel, there's now a better way for you. The principles in this book are proven and tested on thousands of people from all life experiences and with varying desires, but with one core theme:

They want to close the gap between where they are today and where they envision they're able to go.

If you want to do the same, this is your manifesto. If you're here, I'll assume this is not your first rodeo reading books like this—and I'm humbled. My mission is to give you a new perspective, release the immense pressure you've put on yourself, and give you a system you can use for the next year or decade, or for the rest of your life.

Your time is now because there is no such thing as "perfect timing." If you're reading this, it's for a reason—and we have no time to waste.

CHAPTER 1
The Myths

You've been lied to.

SportsCenter, Instagram, Hollywood award shows, even those unbelievable wedding photos captured with just the *right* lighting. It's the seemingly candid social media image created only after 31 takes and painstaking edits. It's your favorite actor or actress strolling down the red carpet.

All of these examples represent a simple, yet precarious reality:

We're obsessed with the highlight reel of life.

Whether it's the fourth-quarter comeback with less than two minutes left that seals the championship, the end result of an Academy Award–nominated movie, or simply achieving a financial goal, there is a deep-rooted myth that runs rampant in our culture and society:

Success comes in a moment—and can happen overnight.

Furthermore, success looks and feels like what the movies show us—the glitz, the music, the awakening moment where you step into a completely different world. Whether in pop culture, entrepreneurship, or the constant cycle of social media posts, we believe this myth, and it's crushing our self-worth every single day.

It's time to break this myth down once and for all. Once you do, you'll be able to navigate it in a way that serves your goals and outcomes. It'll also set you up for realistic expectations and the right amount of intensity and long-term consistency, so you can achieve your wildest dreams.

However, there's also an alternative—to stay where you are:

Stuck, frustrated, and waiting, hoping, and praying something changes.

No, thanks.

We begin our journey by examining the core myths we've been led to believe about success and achievement, why they're obstacles, and how the 1% Rule obliterates them once and for all.

THE EXPECTATION MYTH

Imagine you and I decide we're going on a road trip from Arizona to Venice, California, to meet friends for some exploring and hanging out on the beach, and I'm driving. The gas tank is full, the sun is shining, and you better believe we have a rocking playlist to sing our lungs out to. We're headed out on a journey and we're expecting to get there in six hours.

It's a straight shot, but there's always traffic as we get closer to California. Anything within an hour on either side would seem realistic and possible for this trip. We're pumped, and we're already making plans for what's going to happen once we get there. Our mind's eye has decided this is the narrative we're going to step into, and we couldn't be more excited.

However, reality has a different take:

You didn't sleep well last night and when I pick you up, the energy is low. We get started on the trip, you're fumbling around, and we realize you forgot your wallet. We backtrack 25 miles, and you can cut the tension in the car with a butter knife.

We finally set off, and the first 100 miles are smooth, but then we hit a massive accident. We've barely gotten started and the traffic is bumper to bumper. Worse, I was supposed to change a tire my mechanic warned me about a few weeks back and now it feels off. There's a ringing noise vibrating through the entire car.

Fast-forward four hours, and we're sitting in a mechanic shop in Centennial, Arizona. We look at each other on the verge of exhaustion.

This *isn't* what we expected, and we consider turning around and calling it quits.

This simple story highlights the issue we're all facing in a highlight-reel culture:

Our expectations are sky high, and we're prone to giving up at the first sign of struggle or obstacles.

When we're setting out to launch our new business, it's much like the road trip. We're going wild (did someone say kitchen air-guitar session?) at no longer having a boss and having complete freedom. We're inspired to create our brand, product, or service, and hit the ground running because it's *ours.* We're consuming content telling us we have to simply dream and believe, and we'll achieve anything we want. We're on fire. We *expect* to replace our corporate income in four months or less, to the tune of $6,500 per month for our new business.

We've got some expectations, and we're excited to make them real.

Eight months go by, and we're deep-diving into our savings account. We haven't even made $6,500 during that *entire* period. Our zest and appetite for freedom is replaced by the angst of paying bills and saying no to weekend trips with our best friends. Gone are the days of knowing we'll be paid next Friday and being able to splurge on that new outfit, and we wonder if this is even for us anymore. One of our friends notices our palpable stress and tells us it's time to go back to the "real world."

We decide they're right and throw in the towel. **We give up and give in because our reality didn't match our expectations.** We justify our sky-high expectations by blaming others for our lack of results.

THE BE-ALL, END-ALL MYTH

We can all relate to the prior example because we've been there. We experienced the same reality when we bought a new fitness program expecting to create a strong, lean body or when we wanted to feel enlightened after a week of meditation practice. **We've all given up when our results didn't match our expectations.**

The repercussions of giving up and giving in can be massive and life-altering. Over the course of studying thousands of people who have achieved in ways most people consider out of this world, I noticed a common tendency crucial to the ethos of the 1% Rule. This came up time and time again, almost to the point where it seemed to be a prerequisite to success and achievement:

The first iteration of your goals is never the end result—the magic is in the pivot.

The first iteration of your goals is never the end result - the magic is in the pivot.

THE 1% RULE

We all believe that growth, success, and achievement in life are linear—inputs equal outputs, right?

Wrong. Our entire life experience tells us otherwise. Life is not linear, it's messy, unpredictable, and chaotic. When we're in the middle of this mess, everything is cloudy, and we question what the hell we're doing. Yet a few weeks or months or maybe even a year down the line, we wake up and realize everything was perfect exactly as it happened.

This is why our mechanisms around success are flawed—they don't allow for the fluidity of the pivot essential for finding a more fulfilling path. When I researched the most successful, impactful, and disrupting companies and people, I noticed all of them had experienced a life-altering pivot outside of their expectation.

In the context of business:

YouTube started as a video dating site — discovered people were not looking for dates but wanted to share content, and *pivoted.*

Instagram started as a digital check-in app — discovered people were taking pictures of where they checked in, and *pivoted.*

Flickr started as an online role-paying game app

— discovered people were loving the photo sharing feature, and *pivoted.*

These are massive companies, yet their billions of market share could easily not exist had they expected to get it right the first time. Their expectations were not like the flawless, sun-soaked road trip you and I went on before, but much more flexible to the realities of business and life.

Here's why this matters for you:

Without starting and jumping into the cold water, you'll never clearly see the pivot and the opportunity in front of you, no matter what area of life you're in.

Using the 1% Rule, you'll be able to strategically set expectations designed to serve you and create the awareness of the pivots leading to your ultimate success.

THE PERFECT TIMING MYTH

No one ever wakes up and declares:

I want to feel stuck.
I want to feel overweight.
I want to feel disconnected.
I want to feel sluggish.
I want to feel stressed about money.

Nonetheless, when we look around, we see the stark reminders of our current reality. It's not fun. It's a reminder of what we *haven't* done, how time is passing us by—and how far away we are from where we want to be.

However, instead of starting today, we wait. We sit on the sidelines, watching life pass us by while the clock continues to tick in the background.

Our obsession with the highlight reel gives us another debilitating illusion:

There's a perfect time to get started—and it's *not* right now.

The feeling of being stuck and spiraling out of control are a direct reflection of this mentality. Since we are already sold on the idea of a highlight-reel moment where you and I walk out on stage following a cloud of smoke and the perfect song plays on cue, well then, **we have to wait for the *perfect* time.**

We've all experienced this. Millions of people wait for the calendar year to switch one digit, and *then* they'll get started. I wrote about this in my first book, *UnResolution*. This keeps us from moving forward in every area of our lives, killing both our momentum and achievement in one fell swoop.

The 1% Rule obliterates this myth of perfect timing and instead *creates* the perfect timing. Since perfect timing is an illusion, then today is the only time—hence, it's perfect.

See what I did there? Hope so, but it goes much deeper than a play on words.

Using the 1% Rule, you'll become the creator of your life. The creator understands the myth of waiting around for the perfect time, and knows waiting around for more money, less stress, and an abundance of free time *isn't* reality.

Instead, they recognize it is up to them to choose it. Not tomorrow, not in January, not at the next weekend seminar, but *today.*

THE CHALLENGE MYTH

There's a crucial moment in any endeavor where we're faced with adversity and have a decision to make. Whether we're looking to catapult our career, write a book, or phase out of the honeymoon period of a new relationship, we've all experienced it.

At that moment, we have a choice. The path of least resistance is quite simple: recognize the adversity as feedback that we can't accomplish what we want and fold. Or we can take the path few are willing to take—recognizing the adversity and ultimately using it as a *catalyst* for the next step.

Although a simple distinction on paper, these two ways of handling adversity represent a stark difference—you either achieve greatness, or you don't.

Seth Godin, a brilliant author and blogger, wrote about this in his book *The Dip* (Godin, 2007). He says it's not a matter of *if* the resistance will come, it's *when*. The Dip, as he conceives it, is what stands between starting out and hitting the peak of the mountain. It represents most of the time we spend in any project or endeavor, full of countless challenges. Those who persist break through to the other side. Godin defines the Dip as:

"The long slog between starting and mastery."

In a world where most see adversity as failure, enduring and breaking through to the other side is rare, and therefore, valuable. This means adversity is not only part of the equation, but a gift and a test designed to see how committed you are to your goals. Most people operate under the illusion that success will be easy, regardless of past experiences, and feel disappointed and move on at the first sign telling them otherwise.

However, the 1% Rule operates in a completely different context:

We will experience challenges, adversity, and chaos at least once every single day. Operating under this ethos allows us to not be surprised, but rather to get *excited* when it comes. We recognize this, knowing our competition will fold when faced with a similar circumstance, as would have our prior selves.

This is precisely why the excitement that comes from setting grand visions at personal development seminars is *fleeting*—because we come back to real life. We're short on sleep, our boss yelled at us, and the new puppy can't control his basic functions.

Using adversity as another tool in your 1% Rule toolkit, you'll become a master of personal certainty in a world of chaos. Even during your most challenging days, **you'll systematically move your life forward with an inner knowing that nothing can phase you, and it's only a matter of time.**

Life and work become a beautiful experience when you arrive at this place, and it's available to you now.

DITCH THE HIGHLIGHT REEL

I now invite you to ditch the highlight reel once and for all. Letting this mindset go will deepen your confidence in yourself, and allow you to focus on what's in front of you.

Now that we've gotten this out of the way, it's time to identify the core mindset you'll be operating under going forward. We'll also ensure this doesn't become simply an insight, but a new way of operating. It's one thing to understand this conceptually. It's another to start rewiring the neurological connections we've created to serve the outcomes we're looking to create.

YOUR TURN

Think about your own beliefs and assumptions, and your obsession with the highlight reel of life. Take a moment to reflect and answer the following question:

Where does believing this myth show up in my life and how can I change that starting today?

CHAPTER 2
The 1% Rule

The greatest motivational tool on the planet is not an inspiring video on YouTube, a dance-party seminar, or visualizing the moment you walk on stage. As we revealed in chapter 1, these common beliefs associated with success are tattooed into our hearts and minds, and often hold us back.

This happens for several reasons, including having false expectations, having a distorted sense of reality, or using failure as proof that you're not worthy of accomplishing your goals in the first place.

However, there's one, undeniable motivational force unlike any other:

Progress—even the perception of it.

When we feel we're moving the needle forward in life,

even a seemingly insignificant amount, we stay motivated. Progress keeps us inspired and on track.

In 2011, *Harvard Business Review* (Amabile and Kramer, 2011) performed an extensive study on motivation in the workforce and what truly makes people tick.

Researchers concluded:

> "Through exhaustive analysis of diaries kept by knowledge workers, we discovered the progress principle: Of all the things that can boost emotions, motivation, and perceptions during a workday, **the single most important is making progress in meaningful work.** And the more frequently people experience that sense of progress, the more likely they are to be creatively productive in the long run. Whether they are trying to solve a major scientific mystery or simply produce a high-quality product or service, everyday progress—even a small win—can make all the difference in how they feel and perform."

This can't be overstated. It is the basis of the ethos behind the 1% Rule.

The 1% Rule stems from this principle and combines it

with the Japanese philosophy of *kaizen*. This philosophy is about continuous improvement over the long haul.

These two come together to create undeniable daily micro-progress. When combined with consistency and time, the compound effect takes over and we not only achieve the most audacious of goals, we go above and beyond our wildest dreams.

THE 1% RULE:

1% PROGRESS + DAILY APPLICATION (CONSISTENCY) + PERSISTENCE (FOCUS) + TIME (ENDURANCE) = SUCCESS.

During the rest of this chapter, we'll be breaking down the main components of this rule, seeing the beauty of its simplicity, and learning how to harness it. You'll see your goals and aspirations through a new perspective designed to inspire and empower. Most importantly, you'll discover why progress is crucial to your mindset and your belief that you can achieve anything you've ever wanted.

WHY IT WORKS

I was sitting at a restaurant inside of a nondescript mall in Houston, Texas, knee-deep in a seminar with one of my mentors, Dr. John Demartini. We'd spent six days, up to sixteen hours a day, on intense work, lectures, and learning about the deep-rooted philosophies of life.

I was spent. My brain hurt from the overload of inputs, and my body was breaking down from the inactivity. I was having a conversation with others at the seminar, when one of them said that after this, he was headed to another event, followed immediately by another immersive one.

Whoa, I thought. I couldn't fathom another event because I needed to execute on what I'd learned.

That's when I discovered there were people using personal development and seminars as an escape, not as a tool to execute and create progress in their life. While I love events and believe they should be a staple for our path of growth, I was stunned to discover what I call *"personal development program hoppers."*

However, I was also part of the problem. I'd go to these events, achieve massive clarity, and stay up until three in the morning full of zest. I'd type out an entire grand plan on the plane home.

Then I'd wake up a few weeks later without any tangible sign of progress. Sure, my mindset had been sharpened, but the inspiration and energy had waned, and I didn't have much to show for it. This pattern would repeat for years.

Each time, I'd make a vow: *this* time, it's going to be different. After years of this on-again, off-again cycle, I began to notice a common trend:

When I focused on small daily actions tied to the larger vision, **I felt invigorated and inspired, and I moved the needle.**

When I focused on the end result and the massive vision I'd created, **I felt depleted and uninspired, and suffered from paralysis by analysis.**

I decided to reverse engineer the vision I had created, bringing it down to the smallest common denominator. It'd have to be so tiny, it'd be impossible not to move the needle. The next day, I'd do the same thing—over and over and over again.

For the first time in years, I started to see the real-world, incredible results everyone at these seminars promised. At the time, I was running a fitness business and we more than doubled our revenue in only a few months. I hired my first employee and committed to a ten-day trip to Costa Rica in order to force myself to systemize and automate my business. I was living my purpose and passion, and turning all the information and wisdom from mentors and coaches into real-world results based on daily progress, or micro-wins.

This was the lightbulb moment. I started to recognize the power of the 1% Rule and applied it to every area of my life. I applied it to hundreds of clients. It worked better than I could have *ever* predicted. The results were astounding. They became the core themes of the book you're reading now.

THE MATH

Fast-forward a half decade later, and I'm still using the 1% Rule every day. I've seen it work firsthand on tens of thousands of people. These people, much like me, were stuck and spinning their wheels prior to using it.

They'd consumed all the content on success, achievement, and mindset, yet much like me in that mall in Houston, had few results to show for it. Sure, they could recite why affirmations were powerful and why most people were failing at their goals, including themselves. They could tell you why accountability is crucial and that you shouldn't get overwhelmed with the *how*.

Yet, their life wasn't a living proof of the principles. Their results were minimal. It was frustrating for them to have the awareness and understand the concepts logically, yet be unable to create them in their lives.

It's the guy or gal who knows everything about fitness and nutrition, yet can't seem to get their own act together.

I started to look at the 1% Rule as less of a concept and more of a science.

It started with a simple question:

If I moved the needle forward 1% in every area of my

life, every single day, what would my life look like in one year?

Simple: *I'd experience a 365% increase across my life.* I don't know about you, but that sounds pretty awesome. *What would a 365% increase across all areas of your life look like?*

If you said amazing, you'd be right. However, this barely scratches the surface. Since life is *not* linear, I had to take into account the power of time, compounding, and exponential growth. Compounding applies in various contexts and transforms incremental growth to exponential growth.

The difference between incremental and exponential is the difference between going from 1% to 2% and growing tenfold. That's the moment where the 1% Rule is truly *unleashed.* If you're consistent long enough and persist through obstacles, you're left with the beautiful force of compounding.

The 1% Rule was officially born:

1% PROGRESS + DAILY APPLICATION (CONSISTENCY) + PERSISTENCE (FOCUS) + TIME (ENDURANCE) = SUCCESS.

This universal force creates exponential growth designed to transcend space and time. It allows us to achieve things we never thought possible. Furthermore, it *collapses time* and allows us to pierce right through it.

Classic texts like *The Slight Edge* (Olsen, 2013) and *The Compound Effect* (Hardy, 2012) detail this brilliantly. While you may notice similarities in philosophy, the 1% Rule differentiates itself by transforming a powerful theory into a system of execution and integration.

Those books are classics, there is no doubt. But I found that people really needed a strategic game plan to incorporate the principles and reverse engineer success, all using a practical daily formula.

What I discovered next blew the lid off my reality.

If we simply move the needle forward in our lives every day by 1%, we'd get to 365% improvement over the course of a year—3.65X better.

This is fantastic but doesn't take into account the power of compounding.

If we move the needle forward in our lives every day by 1% and include enough consistency, persistence, and time, **we have the potential of a 3,700% increase over the year.**

Read that again:

Harnessing the power of the 1% Rule, at worst you're going to create an improvement of 3.65X, but you could potentially create up to 3,700%, or 37X more.

Imagine waking up with physical vitality, energy, stamina, strength, and aesthetics *37X better* than the year prior.

Imagine waking up in your marriage or relationship and your love, passion, connection, and growth is *37X better* than the year prior.

Imagine waking up in your business, and your income, impact, influence, and bank account are *37X better* than the year prior.

Imagine waking up in your spiritual connection to your higher self, deeper and more present, fulfilled and on fire to the tune of *37X deeper* than the year before.

The truth is, you probably can't imagine this right now. It's too big, bold, and intense. Thirty-seven times better than where you are today is a completely different reality where you're on fire in every area of life. You're drenched in achievement and fulfillment. People around you keep asking you for the *secret* because you're thriving, and they feel it every time they're around you.

This is the magic moment, the realization of the power

this rule has on your daily life. Even a 10X improvement from where you are today is a different universe.

Don't take this lightly. Use it correctly, and you will never be the same.

HOW TO USE IT

I know what you're thinking: *this all sounds great*, but now what? I get it. You've consumed your fair share of content centered on success, personal growth, and setting and achieving goals.

You may have even taken a weekend out to go to a seminar or live event, yet six months later you had little to show for it but a dent in your bank account. Each time this happens, you lose some of the critical self-trust required to turn the consumption of powerful information into transformational results.

Now you're here and, conceptually, you get it. It sounds great on paper, right? Anywhere from 365% growth in all areas of life in one year, to 3,700% growth.

Where do we go from here? This is why I wrote *The 1% Rule*. I wanted to give people like you a proven system designed upon building an unbreakable foundation while harnessing the most powerful motivational force—*progress.*

What separates *The 1% Rule* from other texts on compounding is the system. This involves taking the concept down to the ground level and helping you craft a game plan to start *now.* While so many understand the inherent value of compounding, I felt there was a key integration piece missing.

Integration is one of my areas of focus and why my clients come back to me time and time again. Defined on my top-rated podcast, *Resist Average Academy*, integration is the process of going from knowing to doing and, ultimately, to being.

KNOWING, DOING, BEING

Any process of learning can be separated into three buckets: knowing, doing, and being. During this powerful process of integration, we take a concept from something we know to something we do, until, ultimately, it is who we are.

Integration is the missing link in most personal development, success, and mindset texts. Without it, we stay stuck in a world of intellectually knowing—but nothing else.

Here's a breakdown of each bucket:

Knowing: an insight, a spark, a concept—simply a starting point. For example, you intellectually *know* how to launch a million-dollar business, drop on a wave to surf, or communicate with confidence.

Doing: the chasm of endless reps, practice, challenges, and adversity. This is where you put all your knowing into practice—and it's hard. It's supposed to be. Most people quit here before they get anywhere near the next phase.

Being: where the magic happens. You are no longer the logical concept. It's who you are. It's being on the wave and not thinking because you've transcended it. It's the way you walk into a room or hold space in a conversation. This is where flow states happen.

Consider these as phases in your evolution as you grow and expand. If you're accumulating endless information, you're clearly in the knowing phase. If you've paired it with practice and daily reps, you're in the doing phase. If you've put in the work for years and have become *it*, you're in the being phase.

Now, these phases can exist simultaneously and will repeat themselves as you expand to new levels. Mastery, then, requires repeating the cycles of knowing, doing, and being as you deepen your skill.

While too "in the weeds" for the context of this book, we'll be referring back to the process of integration. The goal is to supercharge this process while giving you a strategic blueprint for consistently living in a world of doing and being.

Along the way, we'll be taking your grand vision and breaking it down to a level where you can't help but execute.

THE CODE

While the 1% Rule is a powerful concept, it can easily stay as something that sounds great on paper. As I've mentioned earlier, that would be a failure on my part as an author if you weren't able to harness this concept and create real-world tangible results you can both *touch* and *feel.*

It's why I created a code around the 1% Rule, a set of unifying principles to help ensure you maximize every part of the concept. The code becomes the compass pointing to where you're headed and allows you to stay grounded about why you're doing it in the first place.

We'll dig deeper into the Code in chapter 4, including:

1. **Fall in love with the process.**
2. **Do it every single day.**
3. **Celebrate your commitment.**
4. **Track your metrics and data.**
5. **Master your craft.**

YOUR TURN

Setting an intention for anything we do here in life is crucial, and it's your turn.

What has held you back from implementing powerful information you've consumed and what are you committed to doing differently using the 1% Rule?

____

____

____

____

CHAPTER 3
The Possibility

There is no shortage of content, books, blogs, and podcasts about creating a successful, powerful life. We can turn anywhere and find this information at the tip of our fingertips.

However, if you grabbed a random person off the street and asked them the following questions, the answers wouldn't be impressive, and could even be depressing:

How fulfilled are you with your life today?
What is your vision for your life the next three years?
How inspired and excited are you in this moment?
How connected do you feel with yourself and others?

We now have more access to life-changing information, but we have fewer results to show for it than ever. We've never been more connected, yet disconnected. We've never been so ambitious, yet so stuck at the same time. We've never had more opportunity, yet been held hostage to paralysis by analysis.

It's paralyzing.

Over my years as a breakthrough coach, leading individuals, groups, and consulting businesses to break free from the obstacles in their way, I noticed a common pattern:

Most content, coaches, or consultants start by stacking on a shaky foundation.

They take someone who is already stressed, anxious, and running around in life with no strategic plan, no clarity, no vision, and they stack more on top of them. Whether this comes in the form of habits, rituals, or activities, it's a strategy doomed to fail.

When you're already overwhelmed, adding more to your plate will lead to the foundation crumbling. It's simply unsustainable given our limited amount of bandwidth and energy.

We've all seen and felt this before. During the first few weeks of a new initiative, we're able to follow through. We're loving the newfound sense of possibility and results and, because it's new, we've got the dopamine hit of a new routine. However, our brains are masters at making the novel routine, and we begin to notice a downtick in enthusiasm. Every day, energy starts to fade.

We're no longer pumped, and the process starts to take hold. Since we added to a shaky foundation, we're a ticking time bomb. We cling on, but time continues to pass. A few months later someone asks us about the getting-back-in-shape endeavor, the side hustle, the book, the content platform, or relationship goal we had, and we simply respond:

"Oh yeah...*that* thing. I've moved on."

Does this sound familiar? I know it does, because you're here. We've all experienced it, and it's my intention to ensure it never happens to you again.

UNSHAKEABLE FOUNDATION

When you're in the process of buying a home, you rarely ask about the foundation. You don't inquire about the quality of the soil, the water that fills it, the concrete underneath. You don't ask about how it was created or which methodology was used to cultivate the foundation.

You don't really care, but you know it's important. Much like an iceberg, the foundation represents the core structural part of the home designed to withstand the test of time. It's designed to ensure your home survives seasons, changing weather patterns, storms, and more. This is ultimately what will *make or break* the home. The foundation either sets it up for long-term success so it can be a place that families call home, or it can be another project gone wrong.

Yet most people, when setting up their own lives, want to skip the foundation. They want to build out the home theater room before they plot, move, and integrate the soil. They want to focus on the interior design, the feng shui, and the angle of the dining room table, with the art to match. They want to make sure the kitchen has all the bells and whistles.

These are all sexy, they're fun, and they're incredibly exciting.

But much like the weekend seminar and the spark of inspiration we receive, they're ultimately worthless unless we've laid down a powerful foundation and stacked up a well-built plan.

Let's be honest here.

It's not a matter of *if* chaos is going to hit—it's a matter of *when.* We can have a well-thought-out backup plan, but you and I know life will throw us curveballs time and time again.

It'll be testing our grit, fortitude, desire, commitment, and, ultimately, our foundation. When this happens, we either become stronger with our foundation, knowing we weathered the storm, or weaker, folding and caving in to the external challenges.

The 1% Rule was designed to build an unbreakable, undeniable foundation for your life, stacking brick after brick until you've got a masterpiece.

If you decide to trust the process and embrace the daily consistency required to build the foundation of your dreams, you'll experience a shift in your life. You'll create an environment where there's a deeper sense of *knowing*, **a grounded, rooted confidence and certainty about your path and how all your dreams are slowly coming to life.**

It's more powerful than confidence, and it's built on an inner humility few successful people have. But it's right there in front of you, waiting to be captured. The foundation won't sell books, and it certainly won't be trending on Instagram. That's the point, because we know that doesn't work. Without it, however, you'll perish along with your goals and aspirations.

DO IT DAILY

One of the main reasons the 1% Rule will obliterate other forms of goal setting and achieving results is simple:

You're required to move forward every single day.

This may be a challenge for you if you haven't embraced this mindset in the past. It will, with utmost certainty, require you to continue moving forward by 1% on the days you're not feeling like it. In fact—I'll be honest—most days you probably *won't* feel like it. You'll want to sleep in a little longer, slack off on your fitness, and wait to launch your business project until tomorrow.

I'm not here to tell you it's going to feel amazing. However, if it's truly important to you, you'll do it every single day. Since the 1% Rule is about your life, I sure hope it's important to you. I trust you've already figured out how special and fleeting this experience is.

John Grisham is one of the world's most prolific authors with over 45 titles to his name. You can find him taking over serious real estate in any of the remaining bookstores. Even when he was barely starting out and working as a young lawyer, he was harnessing the 1% Rule.

John Grisham committed to writing at least one page per

day, no matter what happened. It didn't matter if he had a long day at the office, or he lost a pet—he committed. He made a decision and chose to follow through. While writing 45 titles and an average of 1.4 books per year seems daunting to anyone who's attempted to write, Grisham broke down the enormous task at hand to the simplest common denominator.

Writing a piece on writing tips for the *New York Times* (Grisham 2017), he elaborates:

"Write a page every day," he advises at the top of a list of eight writing tips he published in the New York Times *recently. "That's about 200 words, or 1,000 words a week. Do that for two years and you'll have a novel that's long enough. Nothing will happen until you are producing at least one page per day."*

This is the 1% Rule in full force, the foundation being built day by day. If it's important, you'll follow through and persist. You'll push through the moments you're overwhelmed and it's a rainy Tuesday morning and you truly don't want to do it.

LOVE WHO YOU'RE BECOMING

Imagine walking into an NFL training camp during the dog days of summer and stopping practice. You huddle up with the coaches, and you tell the players there's something special coming. The players are instructed to take a knee and wait. Then, a covered object is wheeled out from the back of the locker room and onto the practice field.

The players have no idea what is happening—and then the Vince Lombardi Trophy is unveiled. The prized possession, the one thing every single player has dreamed of, is now staring back at them. The most celebrated trophy in all of American sports is right there in all its beauty.

In this imagined scenario, what do you think would happen? Would the players lose themselves in a flood of tears and emotions, hugging and jumping, unable to control their enthusiasm for the trophy?

No, they wouldn't. While I have no doubt they'd be excited, they'd know they hadn't earned it. They'd know it didn't represent the ups and downs of an NFL season. It didn't represent the adversity, the sweat pouring down their faces, the sleepless nights thinking about getting cut, staying in on the weekends to study, and all the doubters, haters, and critics along the way.

In this case, it'd be another shiny object, having lost all its value.

This story represents a simple lesson in life:

We only truly value that which is *earned*—and specifically, that which we earn through the process of becoming.

Notice the words used there: earned, process, and becoming. Without these essential prerequisites, we don't assign precious value to our goals and outcomes. Which means wanting it easy isn't only an illusion, it's a terrible strategy.

According to multiple studies, about 70% of all lottery winners end up going broke and filing for bankruptcy. It's because they didn't earn it or have to change who they were to achieve the monetary success of winning the lottery. Creating financial abundance in life isn't easy. It requires work, persistence, and a changing of one's mindset.

The 1% Rule is about stepping daily into a version of yourself that's already out there. This version of yourself already has all the goals you're desiring, and you're simply taking one step toward making that real today. It's about the process of becoming, slowly going through a metamorphosis.

Which means when you get there, you will have become someone different than who you are today. Inherently, that means you'll have to go through change, and part of change is being uncomfortable. When you truly love who you're becoming, you become unstoppable.

FAITH IS A MUSCLE

To get started with the 1% Rule, you've got to take the leap. The leap is the gap between where you are today and where you want to be in your life. Taking a leap in life is incredibly difficult, and not for the faint of heart. Here's why:

We'd much rather stay in what's known and uncomfortable—even if it's painful. We're afraid of the unknown, and we lack the courage to step into it with faith. Our world can be spinning in chaos and mediocrity, but we won't be compelled to change because it's familiar. Some would say we can become addicted to the frustrations in our life and are receiving a benefit from them.

What you must consider is that your current vantage point

is *limited.* The success you're dreaming of won't hold a candle to what's truly possible for you.

Once we see the unknown through the frame of unlimited possibility, a place where anything can happen, we open up our world. We start to see the unknown as exciting, not something to be afraid of. We take more chances and have the time of our life doing so.

During the process of coaching hundreds of people, I've noticed most people will do nearly anything to avoid taking the leap. These leaps in life are about making bold decisions in the moment, without any guarantee on the other side. It's the moments where you know what to do, but are trembling in fear.

It's not about the size of the leap, it's stepping into it with trust and faith.

For example, the leap may look like:

- » Committing to your side hustle, once and for all.
- » Quitting your job and pursuing your true purpose and passion.
- » Moving to a new environment, a new city on the other side of the country.

» Taking the trip and adventure that calls your heart, even if it doesn't make sense.

» Asking him or her out, even when it feels uncomfortable and the "timing" doesn't feel perfect.

» Following through on the business pivot that calls your heart, but you've been putting off.

All of these require faith, trust, and a detachment from the external world. The truth is, you've always known what to do in the moment, especially when you're listening to your heart and not your head.

But here's the problem:

The big leaps will never happen if we don't get used to taking the small ones. Faith is a muscle that must be built and developing any kind of muscle requires *repetition*. The 1% Rule was designed to help you build this faith every single day with micro-leaps and commitments, so when the high-stakes moments in life appear, you'll be ready.

Furthermore, since the 1% Rule is built around cutting out distractions and getting tuned in, you'll begin to improve your internal signaling system. The more you clear these airwaves, the more you'll trust yourself to know what to do in any given moment. You don't need more time, research, analysis, waiting, sitting on the sidelines, making lists of pros and cons, and feedback from friends.

Instead, using this system:

You'll know what to do in every moment because you've built an inner trust with yourself.

You'll know without a shadow of a doubt what your inner signaling system is telling you to do, and you'll begin to create a powerful dynamic of listening to it in the moments where it doesn't make sense. As time passes, you'll realize the power of operating in life with this rare, yet highly valuable self-trust and self-reliance.

YOUR TURN

Take inventory of your life today—without judgement, narratives, or excuses. One of the most powerful moments in life is the one where you get honest about where you are. You'll be referring back to this section once we get into the trenches of designing the 1% Rule for your everyday life. For each area of life, give yourself a score of 1-10. 1 would be crisis, 10 would be on fire.

NOTE: *The one number you aren't allowed to pick for this exercise is 7.*

Here's where I am in my health, fitness, vitality, and well-being (1-10).

6
____

Here's where I am in my business, income, impact, and influence (1-10).

2
____

Here's where I am in my relationships, social capital, and connection (1-10).

____

Here's where I am in my spiritual and higher sense of purpose with myself (1-10).

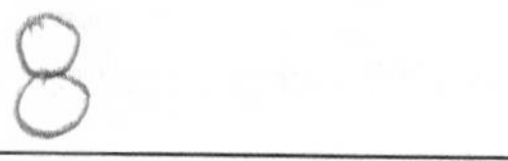

CHAPTER 4
The Code

The samurai were Japanese warriors who were known for their fearlessness, power, and strict code of conduct. They were masters at discipline and fighting, but also the creative arts of writing, painting, and philosophy. They ruled Japan for more than 600 years, from the middle of the twelfth to the nineteenth century.

What separated the samurai from the rest of the population was following a strict code, what they called *Bushido.* These eight virtues were more important than any other part of life and built the foundation for one of the world's most elite warriors. Without a code—a foundational philosophy of virtues and values—we crumble. If we don't have the foundation to lean back on during times of chaos and stress, it's easy to be overwhelmed.

The 1% Rule has its own code, one rooted in the principles to be followed and reminded by when the chaos and stress hit. As we've mentioned earlier, our lives are not linear, nor do they allow a predictable blueprint. Many texts in the personal development sphere have great intentions but seem to be written for robots or artificial intelligence.

You and I will experience endless amounts of human emotion, stress, uncertainty, and chaos as we set about to achieve our goals and targets. The 1% Rule operates with the understanding these things will happen. Having a code grounds us in certainty and clarity around why we're here in the first place, while ensuring we're going to last the test of time.

The alternative is simply repeating the same patterns over and over in life. We'll be much like the ship that takes the voyage out to sea, yet gets stuck in a whirlwind of storms and never makes any tangible progress. The code is your guiding light, it's the beacon to keep you grounded throughout the challenges.

Living the code is a reminder of where your intention, focus, and limited energy go on a daily basis, and it's designed to withstand even the most brutal of storms.

INDECISION, THE DREAM KILLER

Living by a code ensures simplicity along your path. You'll always know what your foundation is and what to rely on. Ultimately, it serves several purposes, one of the most powerful being the ability to cure a behavior pattern we're all guilty of: indecision.

Indecision costs us more than we can ever imagine. This alarming cost includes time, energy, resources, stress, and the constant wasted bandwidth of overthinking. As we move forward with our dreams, we're already overwhelmed with logic, reasoning, and trying to figure out "how."

Barry Schwartz, psychologist and author of *The Paradox of Choice: Why More Is Less* (Schwartz 2016), studied the correlation between endless choices and happiness. He concludes that indecision may be making us miserable, saying:

> "Unfortunately, the proliferation of choice in our lives robs us of the opportunity to decide for ourselves just how important any given decision is."

Let's take a vegan at a restaurant. When the menu arrives, they've already discounted 80% of the potential options. As they go through the menu, they don't even consider the plates with meat. It's as if they don't exist. They simply zone in on the choices in line with their underlying code.

This makes their life *easy*—no back and forth between dishes. There's no overanalyzing and spending their precious energy on best- or worst-case scenarios. Vegan eating, then, is simply an example of having a strict code in life to guide us.

The 1% Rule has its own code, which we'll unpack during the rest of this section, and it will become your foundation to lean back on.

1. Fall in love with the process.
2. Do it every single day.
3. Celebrate your commitment.
4. Track your metrics and data.
5. Master your craft.

The 1% Rule

1: FALL IN LOVE WITH THE PROCESS

Jon Acuff is the *New York Times* best-selling author of several books, including *Start* and *Finish.* A master researcher on goal setting, I asked him what the most difficult day for people who set goals is. Most assume it's the first day when they get started, or possibly the last few days as they push to finish. When I asked Jon (Acuff 2017), he said:

"Simple—Day two is the hardest day and where we see the most drop off."

Shocking. We'd think we'd at least make it a few weeks before experiencing challenges. But Jon's immersive research supports his claim. As I mentioned at the start of the book, we've become a culture, society, media, and business landscape obsessed with the highlight reels of life. Giving up on day two tells us everything we need to know.

We've already identified how this has hurt us individually and as a collective, which is why the first part of the 1% Rule is all about embracing every part of the process. Furthermore, it's about falling in love with the process. Once we do, we're able to put our limited physical, mental, and emotional energy into it with everything we've got.

The process is the metamorphosis of who you've been to who you're becoming.

Without this foundational principle, we'll crumble. Inherently, the process involves challenging moments, breakthroughs, and everything in between. If we expect these to happen, they won't divert us, and we'll keep sharpening our sword every single day.

2: DO IT EVERY SINGLE DAY

The second part of the code is simple: do it every single day—no matter what. As long as we're moving 1% daily, we harness the incredible powers of the rule. It's less about the size and duration of the progress and more about the fact that we're making progress that counts.

There are things you and I already do every single day because they're important. We shower (at least I hope), we brush our teeth, we tell our significant others we love them, we fire up our computer, etc.

At first glance, committing to doing something every single day can seem daunting, but it's the opposite. It takes the pressure off and allows us to flex the muscle of consistency. After years of watching people set outcomes, I've noticed the number one thing standing in their way wasn't the know-how, the plan, a strategy, information, the economy, their environment, relationships, or anything else external.

It was themselves. They would get in their own way.

Many times, they'd give up right on the cusp of a massive breakthrough. Dan Millman (Millman 2017) celebrated author of seventeen books, including the blockbuster *Way of The Peaceful Warrior*, explained this as he told me a story about learning to ride a unicycle for his sixtieth birthday:

"When I turned 60, I wanted to do something special, so a friend loaned me his unicycle. At first, it felt impossible, and humbling. I would practice every day for three weeks, no matter what. What I noticed was there were days where everything fell apart—*crisis days.* I was worse than the day before and it was discouraging, but then I realized the day after the so-called bad days, I made a breakthrough. If you stay with it when it gets hard, you can have breakthroughs to new levels in all areas of your life."

We've all experienced what Millman details with his example of the unicycle, the days we simply want to quit.

In the moment, we feel lost. If we can weather the storm, there's progress waiting for us on the other side.

By living this part of the 1% Rule code, we become the creators of our lives instead of the reactors. We don't live conditionally, waiting to *feel* inspired, excited, and ready. We simply move forward every single day, even if it's an inch or two, and flex the muscle of progress and consistency that only gets stronger with time. Then one day, after enough reps, it simply becomes who we are.

3: CELEBRATE YOUR COMMITMENT

A crucial part of the code is celebrating our wins, even the small, seemingly insignificant ones. Emphasis is on the word *seemingly*, because the size and scope of the win doesn't matter—it's the fact you won, and it must be acknowledged.

Every year, the NFL plays sixteen weeks of regular season football, followed by three or four more weeks of playoff football culminating in the Super Bowl. There are no brownie points or extra credit when you beat a team 20-19 due to a dropped pass in the end zone versus a crushing defeat at 45-3.

While the review of the film and the training in the next

week's meeting room may vary by degree, the win is what matters. In your life, you're experiencing wins every single day, most of which go unnoticed or unacknowledged. Celebrating your wins gives you jet fuel to keep going and extends a token of appreciation for how far you've come, instead of focusing on what's missing.

Every single day, we celebrate a win we experienced as we use the 1% Rule. These micro-wins create the momentum and clarity required to get us to the more expansive wins and outcomes we're chasing. They force us to open up our awareness, and we feed our inner hero instead of our inner critic. They remind us to not judge ourselves and instead appreciate our growth.

4: TRACK YOUR METRICS & DATA

The fourth pillar of the code is to track your metrics and use data to your advantage. Although this part of the code won't light you up with inspiration, it's essential to clearly see the inputs and outputs of our work. Without tracking, we live in a fantasy, which makes decision-making, pivoting, and knowing what's working or not a nightmare.

If we don't have accurate data, our emotions and feelings start to take over, and we base our decisions off those.

While emotions and feelings serve a purpose, they're always changing by default and can't be relied on.

Our feelings and emotions are like the ocean tide, while data and metrics are more like mountains. Peter Drucker famously said: *"If you can't measure it, you can't improve it."* In this context, it's never been more relevant and true.

Have you ever wondered why Weight Watchers is one of the most successful weight loss programs on the market today? To the tune of 1.1 million in-person subscribers and another 1.5 million online subscribers with over 32,000 Weight Watchers meetings happening around the world, they've got a grip on a heavily competitive market.

It's not their points program, their diet, their philosophy, or exercise recommendations. It's a focus on metrics and data combined with extreme levels of accountability, including tracking dietary points, weight, and the percentage shift of BMI (body mass index.)

With this level of showing up and accountability, plus the metrics, it becomes easy to create a strategy and game plan as we grow. For the 1% Rule, we track data to clearly see how far we've come, where we are today, and what strategic pivots or changes we need to create to maximize our success.

5: MASTER YOUR CRAFT

The last part of the code represents a commitment to mastery, and specifically, mastering your craft. While this may sound daunting, it's not. It allows for the patience to develop the crucial components it takes to achieve success in life. Mastering your craft in itself is a long-term commitment and caters to a mindset of grounded humility where you become obsessed with micro-improvements.

Regardless of what your craft may be, the mindset and components of mastery are proven to transcend skill and scope. While the 1% Rule will be used for every part of your life, your ability to focus on a specific craft will separate you from your competition.

In an instant-gratification, highlight-driven, shallow-work world, your pursuit of mastery puts you heads and shoulders above the others and stands the test of time.

This concept of mastering your craft has some crucial components, including:

Deliberate practice:

Pursuing mastery means you'll be practicing. Specifically, you'll embrace *deliberate* practice. Made famous by Daniel Coyle in *The Talent Code* (Coyle 2009), this means pushing yourself to the edge of discomfort during practice to the place where you want to give up. It's easy to practice a skill and do what we're good at. Can you instead spend the time on what challenges you?

Invest thousands of hours:

Mastery takes time, there's no way around it. Expect to invest in thousands of hours to deliberate practice as you sharpen your skills. Whether it's mastering communication or marketing, there's no shortcut to get you there. Sure, there are ways to speed up the process, but don't believe the hype. Embrace this, as most won't do the work required.

Long-term consistency:

It's easy to invest time and effort in a skill when it's new. Once you start to become decent at it, it can become boring. Embracing this and pushing past to a place where you endure will make you invaluable to any marketplace.

A fair warning: don't get all stressed about picking your one pursuit of mastery. For example, my pursuit of mastery is communication—written, audio, verbal, and video. Because these blend into one another, I'm able to commit to a long-term practice under the umbrella of communication.

Choose one and step into it every single day:

You can truly become an expert in nearly anything in a few years, if you focus and embrace the code. An emerging technology can be yours to master, if you're willing to put in the work. This foundation will keep you grounded, focused, and excited to continue to sharpen your mindset and skills on your journey.

YOUR TURN

As you look at each part of the code, start to ask yourself where you feel you could use the most focus and improvement.

Below, identify which part of the code needs your attention, and one action step to integrate it into your experience.

I need to start with falling in love with the process, that's the biggest struggle right now.

CHAPTER 5
The Power of Focus

"A warrior is an average man with laser like focus." - Bruce Lee

Over the course of the last half decade, I've been to countless events.

I've attended everything from the pump up, motivational shot of Red Bull events to the in-the-trenches ones. Each has given me gifts: perspective, mentorship, energy, or simply the opportunity to be surrounded by a like-minded tribe looking to succeed.

However, I've noticed a common pattern: the same people show up to the same events, without much to show for it. Time would pass between events, we'd see each other six months or two years later, and they'd still be spinning their wheels. Not everyone of course, but after seeing this pattern repeat itself, I came to the stark realization:

It's not the quality of our skills that stops us.
It's not the quality of the information that stops us.
It's not the know-how or the inspiration that stops us.

Without a doubt, the number one obstacle standing between people and their dreams is a lack of focus.

In a super-sized, caffeinated, smartphone world, this is obvious. Recent studies show we're now spending an average of 10 hours and 39 minutes in front of some type of screen every day. We've never been pulled in more directions, yet we're going nowhere. When you ask someone how they're doing, they'll never answer:

"I'm so *not* busy. I've got so much free time—this is unbelievable!" However, you and I know there's a difference between a *busy* day and a productive, fulfilling day. We've all experienced a day where we were extremely busy, yet nothing got done. The symptoms of these days include feeling scattered, exhausted, and overwhelmed.

In this state, if we were to ask ourselves the following questions, we would quickly realize our busiest days weren't productive at all:

Did I really move the needle forward in my life and business?

Which activities truly mattered and which could be deleted?

Was I moving *myself* forward or just other people's agendas?

During the last few years, I've become obsessed with reframing my own "busyness" and falling in love with distraction-free work. This key chapter of the 1% Rule isn't the sexiest, but it may be the most important for you.

DEEP WORK

I've always been a writer, or at least wanted to be one. Whether I was writing content for my initial blogs, my fitness business, e-mail, copywriting, or anything in between, it's been a passion. In 2015, I decided to write a book. I got hyped up, gave some high fives, and then sat down in a busy coffee shop in Scottsdale, Arizona.

High off inspiration and cold brew, I got to writing. Around fifteen minutes later, the blinking cursor started to take over. I caught myself wanting to be social, and I made excuses to text, e-mail, or do *anything* but write. Needless to say, that version of the book never got to 1,000 words. I conveniently put it on the backburner, and never opened the document again.

At the end of the year, I was exposed to a powerful text that shifted the way I view work, life, and business. This book was *Deep Work* by Cal Newport (Newport 2016), an accomplished professor, writer, and researcher who seems to accomplish more than anyone in his field.

He used examples of those who took deep work to the extreme and extracted themselves from society, including Carl Jung, Benjamin Franklin, and others. I was floored by the distinctions in the book and realized how much I'd been letting the monkey mind control my life.

The core premise is simple: in an ever-distracted and changing world, the ability to engage in deep work makes you rare and inherently valuable. **Furthermore, the quality of your output increases, as does the level of your feelings of purpose and fulfillment.**

Using the concepts and strategies of deep work, I committed to my book and finished the first draft in a matter of months. The more I engaged in these undistracted sessions, the less I felt the need to check the smartphone or e-mail. I created strict rules around both, including no checking of e-mail until 10:00 a.m. and writing a minimum of 1,000 words a day. I'd spend most of my day in airplane mode. I was unavailable for long lunches and random meetings without an agenda.

It wasn't easy, but as time passed it became my new normal. I started to experience a massive shift. Our minds will use any excuse to avoid deep work, but if you harness it, you'll blow the lid open on what's possible for you to accomplish.

SHIFT THE ADDICTION

The elevator in my apartment in Scottsdale, Arizona, is slow. It's not just slow, it's is-this-broken slow. When I have guests over, they're convinced it's going to get stuck and we're going to experience a *Shallow Hal* moment. There are only four floors, so even at this snail's pace, it doesn't take long to get up top. Yet nearly everyone I'm in the elevator with whips out their smartphones as we go up or down.

Or take the grocery store. If there are more than two people in line, you have no option but to start texting or checking last night's sports scores. Whether this is a matter of social awkwardness, impatience, or the constant need of a digital intravenous drip, we're addicted. It's the moment you're consuming content on Facebook, when you click the link to access Facebook again.

Facepalm.

You know it, I know it—we all know it. The cost of this addiction is hardly seen by most, but includes:

Lack of clarity. Stuffing our brains with information 24/7 is a guaranteed way to add layers to the 50,000 thoughts we're having every single day and add to our sense of not knowing where we're headed.

Lack of completion. Our lack of completion in society is a disaster. On a daily level, we have a terrible track record of finishing anything, from a marketing project to last night's dishes.

Lack of fulfillment. Fulfillment is deeply tied with giving our work meaning, whatever that means to you. The addiction to stimulus takes us further away from feeling fulfilled, not closer.

Lack of energy. The mental and emotional toll distraction has on our brains is frightening and exhausting. We're consuming more caffeine than ever, yet producing fewer and fewer results.

While these are all potentially devastating, the greatest cost of this addiction is **your dreams not coming to fruition**. At first glance, one distracted day may not seem like much. We tell ourselves that tomorrow things will change—and nothing does.

In 2015, I was at the edge of physical and mental burnout with my young fitness business. In August of that year, I gave myself a massive challenge: to take a trip to Nosara, Costa Rica, for ten days and completely disconnect. And I had to do it by December.

I chose a remote surf and yoga haven that required two hours on a dirt road to reach. The morning after I arrived to the tiny town, I sat down for an espresso. Having just arrived from the blistering pace of the East Coast, I ordered and immediately started to get impatient. The waiter passed me several times. Ten minutes passed, then twenty, and my frustration grew at every moment.

That's when I realized my pace was not their pace. I was here to *slow down*, not continue to speed up. Here I was, tapping my feet like a madman waiting for an espresso in paradise, instead of simply *being*. The next few days consisted of early morning surfing, way too much fresh coconut water, and a lot of staring at palm trees. The first 24–48 hours, I noticed an intense desire for the smartphone. Yet on the second or third full day of being disconnected, I became addicted to not thinking about it or checking it.

By the tenth day, I wanted nothing to do with it. I'd relish the moments staring off in the distance for what seemed like hours. I naively vowed to give up forever. This didn't happen, but it made me aware that, no matter how deep we are in terms of our addiction to stimulus, if we can survive the painful withdrawal period, we can become addicted to presence and focus.

Without focus, the 1% Rule won't provide the results you want. Each individual reading this will have a different approach to focus, and making it work for your lifestyle and business is crucial. In the resources section, I'll share some of my favorite tools to help supercharge your focus to new levels. These are simply tools and will only work if you work them.

The moment you become deliberate and strategic with your focus, everything changes. You'll accomplish more in a 75-minute time block than most people do in one day. You'll feel more inspired from within, knowing you're paving the path yourself and not on someone else's agenda. You'll feel calmer, clearer, and with a sense of purpose. Most importantly, you'll harness the undeniable power of the 1% Rule and become addicted to the progress you're achieving day in and day out. This will serve to keep you going and stand the test of time.

SEASONS OF LIFE

Focus isn't sexy and won't move the needle on this book. It's not surrounded by Instagram models, sunsets, and heart thumping EDM music. Focus is boring. As I type this, it's dark and not nearly 5:30 a.m. I'm sitting in pure silence, and my phone is in airplane mode deep within the nightstand drawer. There is no one at my office in downtown Phoenix.

Yet, I feel on *fire*—because I'm starting my day with intention and laser focus. Once you overcome your withdrawals, you'll notice this too. However, your plan will die if you don't set rules around focus to maximize your adherence and results. Once you have this clarity, everything becomes simple in a complex world.

While these rules can apply to anyone and everyone, customize them as needed for your own life. Ensure you're not simply making an excuse, such as, "Well, I have to check e-mail in the morning, it's part of my job."

Is that *really* true?

If yes, can you push the time back?

If no, have you had a conversation with your boss about it?

If they still said no, did you come up with a 90-day plan on how your ability to harness focus and deep work is going to create intangible and tangible value for them?

Okay, great. We got rid of your excuse once and for all. We will always find a way to rationalize our behaviors in life. There's always a way to break through what you believe to be true about the way you're currently operating.

Now let's dig into the nonnegotiable rules to harness the power of focus in a distracted world.

RULE #1: CREATE RUTHLESS BOUNDARIES

Boundaries *matter*. Without them, you become the doormat to everyone else's agenda—at the expense of your clarity and fulfillment. The way you flip this switch is to create what I call *ruthless* boundaries: nonnegotiable frames to help protect your energy, clarity, and focus at any moment.

Contrary to popular belief, boundaries are not selfish—they are selfless. When you and I protect our energy, it means we have more left over for the people that are truly important to us. This becomes essential in a busy and stressed-out world with limited bandwidth.

Here's how to create boundaries to increase your performance and fulfillment:

Stop checking e-mail all day. The days of the inbox being open all day are long gone and the research proves it. Set a strict time to start checking e-mail. Mine is 10:00 a.m., and I adhere to it 90% of the time, unless a team member needs something sent, and even then, I avoid "checking" it. Sometimes I'll cover the screen with a book to ensure I don't even see the unread messages. A little whacko, but it works.

Start your day on "airplane mode." Cut the crap—you don't need to check stocks or Twitter to start your day. You're robbing yourself of key insights and clarity to help your life and business. My smartphone won't be turned on until seven or eight, and only for meditation and music and to message my soul mate.

Prime your environment for focus. Our brains are designed to set us up for success in any environment. If you're in a loud coffee shop surrounded by people, your brain is going to opt-in to social mode. If you're in a cluttered office, your brain is going to be distracted by messiness. Prime your environment and be creative and ruthless with this. For example, when I'm writing at my office, I'm in a conference room with nothing but my laptop. My phone stays in the main room, tucked deep in my bag.

Boundaries only work if you work them. Communicate with others on what to expect and follow through on them every single day.

RULE #2: DOUBLE YOUR RATE OF SAYING "NO"

The most dangerous word in regard to your focus is *yes.*

The moment you say yes to one thing, you're automatically saying no to something else. As a culture, we have an issue with saying no. It's seen as confrontational. We'd rather say yes to something we know we're going to hate and then cancel at the last second. In essence, we exchange long-term fulfillment for the short-term gratification of pleasing others.

Stop it. Trust me, I used to be the king of the half-hearted yes to invitations. When I was knee-deep in growing my fitness business and working seven days a week, friends would invite me out to town. Deep down, I knew the answer was an unequivocal no, yet I didn't want to disappoint them, so I'd say yes.

After a few months of this, they stopped inviting me. I got the message: I was being a flake, and my yes had zero value to them. Worse off, my yes had zero value to me and I couldn't honor the word of the man in the mirror.

They always knew I'd cancel or not show up. At that time, I didn't have the courage to say no on the regular, but now I do. As someone who runs an interview-style podcast, I've had to become extremely used to high-profile guests saying no over and over. I live in a world of rejection, no matter how creative my proposals may seem.

At first, I didn't love it, but I respected it. I personally get invited to lunch or coffee at least three times per week. This is twelve to twenty times per month. And I say yes to one time every other week, at most. The reason is simple: I'd love to hang back and go to lunch or coffee. However, as a content producer, writer, podcaster, video creator, coach, and entrepreneur, I know myself. The moment I go to lunch, the social part of my brain is at full force, and I'll *never* get back to work.

In other words, my day is lost once I say yes to a lunch. Having this self-awareness in your life is crucial too.

RULE #3: COMMIT TO A PRACTICE

Focus is a *practice*, which means you're building a skill. Much like flexing a muscle at the gym, you get stronger the more you use it. This is why in my coaching and mastermind groups, we have a "purpose" component to our morning routine. It's designed to do one thing for our business to ensure that, even if we have the most chaotic day in the world, we at least moved our business forward 1%.

If you want to harness the power of focus, you have to flex the muscle every single day. This may sound overwhelming, but it's not. If you're starting out, your practice can be as simple as 20 minutes of undistracted deep work. What you choose to do with this time is all on you. Once you've proven you can do this for at least 45 days, add time. I share some incredible resources below and in the back of the book to keep you in check and living the "data" part of the code we described earlier.

When we practice, it's much more important to do it daily for an hour than to do it twice a week for three hours. Duration is less important than intensity and consistency. Practicing means you're in it for the long game, and it's a daily application. Once we understand this, we take the pressure off ourselves and focus on the next step waiting for us. We trade our love for tomorrow for the realities of today. Slowly, you'll start to look forward to this quiet, undistracted *you* time.

TOOLS TO MASTER

Focus requires high amounts of attention and, without tracking, we'll get lost. Ask the average American how productive they feel, and they'll grossly overestimate. The truth is, the average American is productive for two to three hours a day (Crawford 2013).

Yes, you read that right. It's a disaster out there. Between coffee breaks, countless check-ins, interruptions, and open work space, we're laughably terrible at productivity. While an argument can be made that the reason for this is our disconnection from work, the truth is much more complex.

You and I are in the process of rewiring our brains, constantly seeking the next dopamine stimulus—and we're paying a heavy price. The resources section of this book is packed with all the tools I've used to sharpen my sword of focus. They've also been proven with countless others. Below, I'll highlight the most relevant you can start using now to become a master of focus, productivity, and your own version of deep work.

Remember, at the end of the day, these are simply tools. They won't do the work for you or turn off your favorite TV show in the background. They'll work, if you work them.

POMODORO

Take a moment to reflect and answer the following questions honestly:

When was the last time you did any undistracted work?
When was the last time you didn't check e-mail upon waking?
When was the last time you spent a few hours on airplane mode?

If you're like most, the answer is you haven't. But you're reading this book, so take that as a win. Hopefully, it will compel you to action. If all I did was make you feel good, I wouldn't fulfill my mission. One of the most powerful tools I've ever encountered for extreme levels of focus is known as the Pomodoro technique.

The technique was made famous by Francesco Cirilo and

is based on performing 25 minutes of completely undistracted work, followed by a 5-minute break. This would be "one" Pomodoro. After doing four cycles, you'd take a 15 to 20-minute break.

It seems way too simple to most people when they read it, or I teach it. However, for these 25 minutes, you're zeroed in on one task. No e-mail, no social media, no phone, no text, no conversations—nothing but the work in front of you.

There's a reason why this system is so popular: *it works.* There is an art and science to the 25 minutes. By the time you get frustrated and challenged, you're close enough to the finish to stick it out. Once you start accumulating some Pomodoros, you won't want to stop. You will be amazed at your level of output in a couple sessions, and it'll become addicting. You can find resources around this tool in the back of the book.

If you're just starting out, I want you to begin with the smallest possible denominator:

You're going to perform one Pomodoro time block every single day. It doesn't matter who you work for or what you do. Use it for your current career, for a passion, or to sharpen a skill. Don't start with six, that's not realistic.

Start with one and watch what happens during the next 30 days.

As we mentioned as part of the code of the 1% Rule, tracking is absolutely nonnegotiable. It must happen on a daily, weekly, quarterly, and yearly basis for success. Early on, you're going to keep it simple or else you'll fail. In the resources section of the book, I'll list my favorite tools to manage, track, and understand the metrics behind your focus.

Slowly, this will become your secret weapon for tracking your focus.

PAVING THE SUPERHIGHWAY

Before we move on, I want to remind you not be so hard on yourself. You're going to get inspired and excited about what's possible from reading this book. However, you're also going to fight your fair share of resistance.

Let me explain.

Right now, you're operating on a *super highway* of habits, rituals, and ways of operating in life and business. Most of these aren't conscious to you, they're automatic. This highway has been paved and hundreds of thousands of miles have been put on it.

When you're ready to make a change—for example, inserting Pomodoros into your experience and not checking e-mail until 10:00 a.m.—it's going to be hard. When I say hard, I mean *really h*ard. This behavior isn't wired into your brain, so it looks like an unpaved patch of dirt in a third world country.

The neural connections need time to create new pathways in your brain, so be easy on yourself. Remember the core ethos of the 1% Rule. I insert this reminder at the end of the focus chapter because I've taught this system over and over and seen people set ambitious goals only to revert back to their status quo and feel frustrated.

Steady progress will win the race, and slowly you'll start to build a new network of neural connections designed to keep you in focused work for longer durations of time. You'll reap the benefits that come with knowing where you're going and being able to prove to yourself you're on your way.

YOUR TURN

It's time to see where you are in terms of your focus and craft a game plan going forward.

On a scale of one to ten (no 7 allowed), here's my current level of focus on a daily basis in regard to my purpose, mission, business, income, and influence:

____

Here is what happens the first hour of the day, including media consumption, smartphone use, e-mail, and other distractions.

____

____

____

Based on the above, identify and commit to one new practice and behavior change that will make you more likely to have a productive and focused morning or day.

____

CHAPTER 6
Persistence

She became the first author on the Forbes billionaire list by creating one of the most successful book franchises of all time.

However, if we look back, it could have easily never happened. On the verge of personal crisis and considering suicide, JK Rowling (Rowling 2008) was living off government assistance and her world was spiraling out of control.

In her words:

"An exceptionally short-lived marriage had imploded, and I was jobless, a lone parent, and as poor as it is possible to be in modern Britain, without being homeless ... by every usual standard, I was the biggest failure I knew."

Yet, she persisted through countless rejections and committed to the creative process.

Regardless of the chaos in her life, she was able to

experience the quantum success of the Harry Potter series, which led her to wealth, fame, and stardom. If clarity and inspiration get us started, persistence is the grit beneath it all. It's messy and keeps you going long after the high of starting has worn off.

We all know what persistence looks and feels like, but where does it come from? Furthermore, what separates those who have high levels of it and those that fold at the first sign of challenge? Fascinated by this question, I spent countless hours knee-deep in research to extract what keeps some people going, while others quit.

Persistence isn't special and doesn't have to be acquired at a seminar. It's what keeps us waking up early to pursue our dreams. It keeps us fueled when our friends and family tell us it's time to get a "real job" and quit the fantasy.

PERSISTENCE, DEFINED.

Starting is easy. Let's not kid ourselves—new is exciting. It provides endless amounts of the insatiable spark of inspiration. It's the novelty factor—we're on cloud nine, and nothing can stop us. Our brains receive endless hits of hyper-addictive dopamine, and we're on fire.

Whether it's a new relationship, moving to a new part

of town, quitting your job and going solo, or launching a platform, the energy and inspiration are on full force.

However, as you've already experienced, this feeling has a limited shelf life. We're under the illusion we're supposed to feel this way about everything forever, which means we'll quickly give up the moment it's gone. Once the high has worn off and we're faced with a few challenges, we have a decision to make.

The decision is simple and can be identified in the form of a question:

Do you persist and endure, continuously growing though support and challenge?

Or…

Do you find the next "new" thing to latch on to so you can feel the initial feelings again?

There's an allure to rationalizing why a pursuit didn't work and deciding to start all over again. In the entrepreneurial space, we see this all time. It's the person with 9 websites, 24 domains, and 4 different sets of business cards, but nothing to show for any of them. The high off the possibility has intoxicated this individual and has now become an *avoidance mechanism* to doing the real work needed to move their business forward.

Persistence changes all of this and allows us to embrace the full scope of the journey. Angela Duckworth, researcher, psychologist, and author of the book *Grit* (Duckworth 2016), takes the definition of persistence further and identifies it as "grit":

"Grit is the tendency to sustain interest in and effort toward very long-term goals. Self-control is the voluntary regulation of behavioral, emotional, and attentional impulses in the presence of momentarily gratifying temptations or diversions. Grit can be simply defined as **perseverance and passion for long-term goals.**"

Here's what grit and persistence *really* look like:

» The sweat pouring down your face after thousands of practice shots

» Performing the webinar launch when one person showed up (thanks, Mom!)

» The moments in your relationship when you want to run, hide, and call it quits

» The sleepless nights wondering why the hell you're doing what you're doing

- The moments you're driving home and start crying uncontrollably with no rhyme or reason
- The existential questioning of why you can't simply get in line and follow the rules
- The pouring out of your soul with no guarantee of anything in return

And the list goes on. These are the defining moments when you truly discover who you are. While intense, challenging, and tough, grit and persistence are beautiful and will give your journey meaning.

CULTIVATING PERSISTENCE

If persistence and grit are so important in our journey, how do we find it within us and cultivate it to our advantage?

A myth holding people back from creating persistence is that those who have it are simply born with it and can't create it. While there's absolutely a certain level of nature associated with persistence, the decision to create it in your life as a skill and superpower is up to you.

Persistence is created by choosing it time and time again. Every single day, we will experience countless moments of doubt and fluctuations in our physical, mental, and emotional energy, all of which can stop us in our tracks. The cultivation of persistence requires us to detach from the feelings of the moment. Specifically, it's about executing, regardless of what we're feeling—all the time.

The following four essentials are crucial for cultivating your persistence:

I: Knowing exactly where you're going.

As we've mentioned, without clarity, we don't have anything. If we don't know what our long-term vision is, we'll got lost in a sea of distraction and always be looking to start a new project without taking it to completion.

For example, my long-term vision is to be a *New York Times* best seller. I can already see and feel what it's going to be like to walk into a bookstore (if they still exist, of course) and pick up my best-selling book. This keeps me going to write, write, write, and write some more.

This intense clarity—with a deeply rooted *why* that gets me emotional—allows me to endure. It takes a massive goal and puts me in the driver's seat as I become obsessed with the process and nothing else.

In your life, once you have massive clarity on where you're headed, combined with a deep and powerful *why*, you'll begin to unlock the persistence and grit required to achieve all of your wildest dreams.

II: Understanding the inherent challenges.

We grossly underestimate how hard it will be to complete our vision and outcomes. We assume a few challenges, yet we never know what it's truly going to take. There are two types of challenges: the ones in plain sight, and the ones we only encounter once we move the needle and execute. Reframing challenges as opportunities to grow and doubling down on your vision is crucial to flexing the muscle of persistence.

This is not about creating challenges in advance; it's a matter of expectations. If we expect the ride to our dreams to be challenge-free, we're in for quite a surprise and will ultimately give up and give in.

III: Detaching from your feelings.

If you stay with anything long enough, it will get hard and you'll want to stop.

Understanding that your desire to do anything in life will vary minute to minute, day to day, and hour to hour allows you to step away from your feelings. Many times, experiencing doubt and resistance means we're growing, stretching, or in the process of *becoming*. When they come up, smile—and learn to love them.

Feelings are important, but if we let them control our ability to execute and follow through on our goals, we are held hostage and lose our own self-reliance. The moment you learn to execute regardless of how you're feeling, everything changes.

IV: Setting ablaze your deeper desire.

Napoleon Hill introduced the concept of burning desire in his classic text *Think and Grow Rich*. He also dedicated an entire section to persistence, calling it "the sustained effort necessary to induce faith."

Without a burning desire, or a deeply rooted *why*, we'll lack persistence. If you find yourself unclear about where you're headed, that's where your focus must lie.

In order for a *why* to be powerful enough, it must contain certain ingredients. These include powerful emotions that pull at our heartstrings in a meaningful way. In Chapter 9, you'll get hyper-clear on your vision, and you'll see your persistence explode.

HAVE A CHIP ON YOUR SHOULDER

Personal development and spiritual purists are going to disagree with me here, but I believe our ability to persist has to come from both sides of life: dark and light. While the topic of polarity is too expansive and deep for the purpose of this book, it is part of life and a universal law.

The law of polarity states that everything that exists has an equal and exact opposite.

While positive thinking and optimism are beautiful and required for a life of both success and achievement, there are times we must dig into the darker emotions we experience and use them as a creative source of power.

Ultimately, these become a powerful force for persistence over the long term. One of the greatest examples of this comes from Michael Jordan, undoubtedly one of the greatest basketball players of all time.

His persistence was largely fueled by being cut from his high school basketball team and being told he wasn't good enough. This was such a powerful force in his life that, decades later, after five MVP awards and six NBA championships, Jordan still emphasized those who didn't think he'd make it when he gave his Hall of Fame speech. And he went straight after them.

The *Chicago Tribune* expands:

"When Michael Jordan was done Friday night, it's a wonder anybody had eyebrows left, such was the (mostly) good-natured scorching he applied to his friends and foes. His Hall of Fame induction speech turned into a roll call of all the people whose insults, real or imagined, made him the competitor he was." (Morrissey 2009)

I believe we can use this energy wisely, without letting it consume us. It doesn't mean we become engulfed by this dark energy and never release it. Instead, we use it as a launch pad for relentless action, grit, and persistence. For example, when I'm training in the gym, I'm imagining all the people who told me I wasn't good enough or laughed when I declared my dreams.

The truth is, these things don't affect me anymore on a day-to-day basis. However, I *strategically* focus on them and expand them in the moment to amplify their intensity when I'm required to dig deeper and extract a part of myself that isn't accessible only through positivity.

Once I've used this fuel, I wind up at positivity and light anyway, which becomes a beautiful experience. You also have this energy, and I urge you to use it in a productive manner. At the end of the day, it has nothing to do with other people if you've moved on emotionally. They are simply reflections of your own self-critique.

When you use this energy wisely, you're able to recognize the voices in your own head trying to stop you, and ultimately, you overcome them in a powerful way, while building your persistence muscle.

DO YOU WANT IT BADLY ENOUGH?

Plato traveled far and wide as a student and came to see the mentor of mentors, Socrates. Having an unquenchable thirst for knowledge, Plato would do anything to heed his mentor's advice and learn from his wisdom and knowledge.

Plato wanted it *all* and wanted it now, proclaiming to Socrates about his deep desire to have his level of wisdom. Socrates, avoiding his tantrum, simply told him to follow. He walked for a couple miles and approached the ocean. Plato followed his mentor, yet was confused, thinking:

"Why am I out here? What does the ocean have to do with my desires?"

As they walked out into the tide, the water grew more and more intense. First, it was at their shins, then their hips, and ultimately beyond chest level. Socrates paused, piercing his young protégé with his gaze, and asked again:

"What is it you want from me?"

Plato doubled down on his previous answers, saying knowledge and wisdom.

Socrates stood still, holding the energy space for a moment, and walked toward him. He aggressively grabbed the hair at the back of his head and shoved him under the water.

Seconds passed, and Plato squirmed and squirmed, while Socrates kept him underwater. When he was nearly unconscious, he brought Plato out of the water.

"What was that for!? You nearly drowned me. Are you crazy?"

Socrates took a moment, smiled, and simply said:

"The moment your desire for knowledge and wisdom matches the desire you just experienced for air, you will have it."

And therein lies the lesson:

When we truly, deeply, and authentically desire our visions, we will persist in the face of extraordinary challenges. We won't require external motivation; we'll be so driven from every cell of our body that we will simply move forward because we don't know any other way.

The parable of Socrates and Plato provides an invaluable lesson on desire and taking what you want to create as seriously as life or death.

Because here's the secret: it *is* life or death. You and I have nothing guaranteed in this life, and every single day over 151,600 leave this experience of life here on Earth. As Steve Jobs once famously said in a beautiful commencement speech at Stanford:

> "Remembering that I'll be dead soon is the most important tool I've ever encountered to help me make the big choices in life. Because almost everything — all external expectations, all pride, all fear of embarrassment or failure — these things just fall away in the face of death, leaving only what is truly important. Remembering that you are going to die is the best way I know to avoid the trap of thinking you have something to lose. You are already naked. There is no reason not to follow your heart."

You have no excuses. Your time is this moment because it's all we will ever have. Treat it as if it's life or death, because it is.

COMPLACENCY KILLS PERSISTENCE

We've narrowed down what drives and builds the muscle of persistence, but now it's time to address the silent killer. This mindset destroys persistence and leaves you scattered and spinning your wheels:

Complacency.

Complacency is the moment we get comfortable and decide it's good enough. It's the moment we settle and stop growing and challenging ourselves. Persistence thrives on constant challenges and seeking new experiences. If we aren't constantly bumping up against our perceived limits in life, we begin to lose the quest for growth.

Even for those who are "successful," complacency draws the life force out of their veins and sucks away all their enthusiasm and zest for life.

Without constant challenge, we're left frail and without direction. To illustrate how crucial this is, let's look at the concept of retirement. Retirement is a concept created by society. It's a system of growing up, producing, and finally relaxing once all the work has been done and all the money has been made.

During the last decade, retirement has gone through an evolution as markets have changed and many people have woken up to the false sense of security it promises. More importantly, we've recognized the dangers of retirement and that a thriving, energized person with a purpose can turn into a disease-filled person with no zest.

Without a healthy dose of challenge, we wither away and slowly begin to fade. Our physical, mental, emotional, and spiritual capacity is no longer used or tested, and it begins to suck the life force out of us.

We don't have to go through retirement to recognize this. There have certainly been moments in your life where you fell prey to the soul-sucking feeling of complacency.

Here's how to identify when you're on a one-lane highway toward complacency:

You no longer feel challenged.

Challenge increases our capacity, helps us become more, and gives life a deep-rooted meaning. If we examine any organism on the planet, from the tiniest particles to the material of the cosmos, we learn a powerful universal principle:

Maximum growth happens at the intersection of support and challenge.

While we may fight it, avoid it, and resist it, deep down we want challenge because it tells us who we are and provides meaning.

Enthusiasm has started to wane.

Enthusiasm is a creative energy unlike any other. Once you start slipping into complacency, you'll notice your enthusiasm wane. Eventually, it'll turn into boredom—or worse, apathy. Enthusiasm is cultivated through meaningful work and progress.

If you find yourself lacking enthusiasm for anything in life, pay attention. It's telling you bluntly that something is missing, and you've gotten too comfortable with the status quo.

You tell yourself you're in a "good spot."

Good is the enemy of great. The moment you tell yourself and others you're in a "good" spot, or you're "fine," you begin to lose what got you where you are. You rest on your laurels, and you stop growing. It's one thing to feel fulfilled and strategically decide to focus on another area of your life. It's another to use the mask of "good" to stop all momentum.

You begin to lose your drive and ambition.

Drive and ambition are the jet fuel that keep you going over the long term. A sure sign of complacency is losing the spark and not feeling "it" anymore. What makes you tick is always with you, regardless of your success or how stuck you feel at any moment. When ignored, it begins to fade, and one day you'll wake up and wonder how to get it back.

HOW YOU DO ONE THING IS HOW YOU DO EVERYTHING

We've discovered the value of persistence, or grit, and how it's a crucial part of the 1% Rule. Without it, nothing you do will matter because it won't last. Your declarations will turn to entertainment, and you'll be stuck spinning your wheels.

However, it's important to recognize that persistence is a muscle that can and must be worked on daily **and that how you do one thing is how you do everything.**

In a commencement speech at the University of Texas in 2014, William H. McRaven explained this concept in a simple message he gave to those seeking success:

"Make your bed in the morning."

McRaven argues this seemingly insignificant detail starts your day off with accomplishment. You start by fighting the resistance we're all going to experience. By simply committing to action and rising up to the challenge of making our bed, we create a domino effect that leads to us challenging our bodies, minds, and spirits.

This concept is simple:

Your life will show proof of your principles and your deeply rooted integrity.

If you can't build the muscle of persistence during low-stakes situations, it'll become incredibly difficult to show up when the stakes are high.

This quote, originally credited to Greek poet Archilochus, and later made famous by a Navy SEAL, illustrates the point:

"We don't rise to the level of our expectations; we fall to the level of our training."

Luckily, creating micro-challenges as part of your daily routine is deeply imbedded in the ethos of the 1% Rule. You're going to be crafting a game plan to challenge yourself at least once a day. You'll flex the challenge muscle. This sets the tone for the rest of your experience.

YOUR TURN

Based on the above, where can you maximize your level of persistence and grit in your life? Choose one specific area of life and identify how you're going to make it happen.

For example: *I can harness the power of persistence and grit with my physicality. The one way I will make this happen is committing to working out and training three times a week, and I will wake up at 5:30AM no matter what.*

CHAPTER 7
Endurance

You're dialed in and you're focused.
You've developed grit and persistence.
You've cultivated a long-term vision.

While all these will serve you, there's one remaining piece: *endurance.* As Angela Duckworth, author of *Grit* (Duckworth 2016), states:

Enthusiasm is common, endurance is rare.

Endurance is what separates the master from the masses and the amateur from the professional. It separates those who stay focused and persistent on a long enough timeline to watch all their dreams come true.

Endurance is not sexy, it's not flashy. It will include countless moments of doubt and wanting to stop. However, if you last long enough, you'll come out the other side recognizing how this piece of the puzzle puts it all together on your way to the top of the mountain.

Endurance is not only a principle, it's a mindset of commitment. It's one thing to commit for a year. Endurance is committing to a process that lasts decades. In a microwave world, endurance will set you apart and you will inherently become highly valuable in any marketplace.

During this chapter, we're going to deep dive into the power of endurance, learn how to harness it in your life, and ensure it becomes your secret weapon along the way. You'll instantly separate yourself in a surface area world promising how success is right around the corner.

ENDURANCE IS MESSY

Endurance is *messy*—deal with it.

If you've ever seen someone complete an endurance race, you know it's a hard, intense experience and a messy ordeal of mental, physical, and emotional stamina. Just like an endurance race, you're in for a ride when you choose to last. It will be hard and intense and yet incredibly beautiful.

David Goggins, former Navy SEAL, experienced a

tragedy post-retirement and decided to honor his fallen brothers by pursuing one of the most difficult experiences in the world: the Badwater Ultramarathon, 135 miles known as the "toughest footrace on the planet."

There were a few problems. One, Goggins had never run more than a few miles. Two, he was a powerlifter who weighed 280 pounds. Three, to qualify for Badwater, you had to have completed at least one 100-mile event. And so he did.

Goggins had 24 hours to complete his and, somehow, despite excruciating odds, he did it. In his own words describing the last 19 miles:

> *She [his wife] helped me up and we started walking around the track at a 35-minute-mile pace. I asked her if I would complete the 100 miles in 24 hours at this pace and she said no. So I did what I had to do and somehow, by the grace of God, started running again. I completed 101 miles in just under 19 hours. I had broken all the small bones in my feet and my kidneys were failing. My wife drove the car onto the race course and put me into the back of the car. We live on the second floor of an apartment complex and we had to somehow get up the stairs. So, I draped my arms around her neck from behind and she had to practically drag me up the*

> *stairs. After she got me in the shower and she saw that I was urinating dark dirt brown, she begged me once again to go to the hospital. I looked her in the eye and said. . . Just let me enjoy this pain I'm in.*

Sure, an extreme example—but that's endurance to the utmost degree. You will be pushed to places you never imagined, and you're going to have moments when you wonder what the hell you're doing and why you can't simply get in line with everyone else. You'll experience sleepless nights, existential crises, and moments that bring you to your knees.

Understanding the messiness of a committed life is crucial to your success and, ultimately, your ability to endure. Early on in my CrossFit training career, I heard the phrase "embrace the suck." Every workout was going to be hard, no matter how simple it seemed on paper.

(Newsflash: if it seems simple on paper, it will annihilate you in ways you'd never imagine.)

Which meant when I was knee-deep in mental and physical pain, I would reframe the pain and see it as a gift. It became the feedback mechanism that showed I was growing. The illusion that your path and your vision won't have pain is simply that—*an illusion.* It's time to drop that once and for all, lean into the moments where you're at your edge, and choose to step beyond it.

A DECADE OF OVERNIGHT SUCCESS

Matt Damon and Ben Affleck were struggling. They'd been going to auditions and traveling countless miles only to be disappointed when they didn't get the parts they wanted. Young and naïve, they decided to start writing a screenplay during their downtime, fueled by late nights and cheap beer. Years passed, and they kept going. This screenplay ultimately became *Good Will Hunting*, a smash hit featuring Robin Williams. It garnered nine Academy Award nominations, made $236 million, and launched two blockbuster careers.

While they were touted as a massive overnight success, Matt has a different take (Damon 2014):

"When Good Will Hunting *came out, everyone said we were overnight successes. For us, I'd been in the union for ten years and been slugging it out, and Ben for eleven years."*

Behind every overnight success are years of focused effort, struggle, challenge, and rejection. The myth of overnight success plays well in a highlight-reel culture, yet when one pulls back the curtain, it's easy to see the 1% Rule in effect.

Whether it's Elon Musk, Peyton Manning, Gary Vaynerchuk, or your favorite band, once you look deeper, you realize they were all overnight successes of a certain kind:

To achieve overnight success will require a decade of consistency.

It's incredibly easy to take a snapshot out of context. For example, take your favorite musician. Right now, you see them selling out tours, creating records, playing on late night TV, and traveling the world. But this snapshot isn't a one-off picture. It's the thirty-first take.

What you don't see is: *touring around the country in a beat-up van, cramming seven people into a crappy motel, fights with record labels and management, deciding whether to pay for gas or the rent, dealing with haters in their scene who say they are selling out or getting too big, band member drama, questioning life on a random, middle-of-nowhere bench after a flat tire on the van—and countless moments of wanting to call it quits.*

When I read these stories of rejection, struggle, and adversity, I'm empowered. If overnight success was real, you'd have tremendous pressure. Instead, you can focus on taking today's step, understanding that you're building a rock-solid foundation. Understand that at every moment you're crafting your unique story and journey. One day, if you endure long enough, *others will call you an overnight success.* You'll smile with an inner knowing of the intense, riveting, and beautiful journey you've been on throughout that time.

The truth is, if you experienced overnight success, you wouldn't value it anyway. I'm serious. If I showed up to your apartment, home, or office right now with all your dreams and aspirations, you'd undoubtedly be excited. Yet, that would fade quickly because you'd know it wasn't earned.

Remember the example from earlier in the book about the football team that was given the Vince Lombardi trophy during training camp? Same idea. Nothing which isn't earned is highly valued.

YOUR MOUNTAIN IS YOURS

Don't compare your start or middle to someone else's ending, or you'll never endure. In a social-media-fueled, all-access world, it becomes easy to take our evolution and compare it with someone else's.

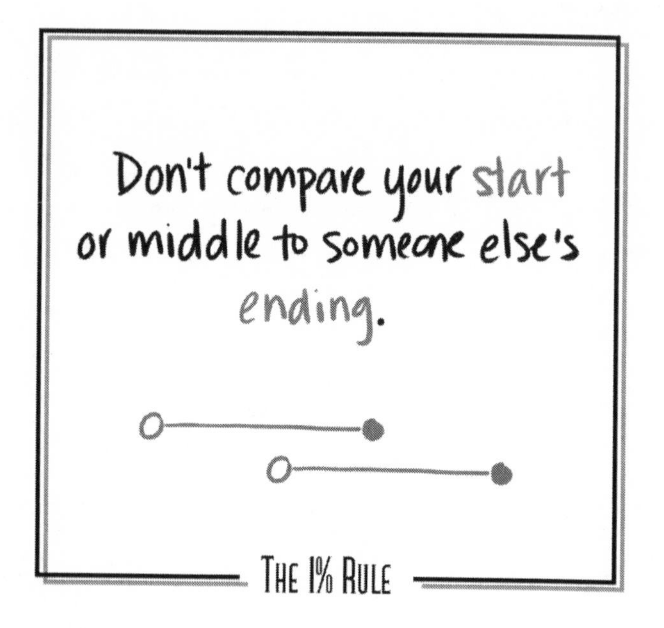

While this can be inspirational and empowering, human nature dictates we'll be focused squarely on what's missing and how far we have to go, instead of what's possible.

Psychologists have long studied comparison, dividing it into two buckets:

Upward comparison is when you and I compare ourselves to someone who we perceive has accomplished more than us, while *downward* comparison is when you and I compare ourselves to others under the perception we've accomplished more than they have.

In a 2006 study (White et al. 2006), researchers discovered the effects of upward comparison: envy, reduced self-esteem, or symptoms of depression. They found we tend to simplify and forget the complexity of other's lives, and we rationalize why they were able to experience success that we haven't. Many times, this rationalization lets us off the hook.

We've all done it. For example:

"They got lucky, and they're not talented."

"They came from money, so everything is easy for them."

"Their parents must have connected them to that person, and that's why they're successful."

This perception is highly disempowering and can be reframed to show us what's possible for our own lives. Remember: your mountain is *yours*. Your journey is one-of-a-kind and will never happen again. Your exact mix of background, environment, family, brain chemicals, and way of viewing the world is 100% unique.

One powerful tool I've used is simply humanizing all the people in our industry we look up to. For example, if you are starting a social media marketing plan for yourself or a brand, product, or service, it is easy to look at Gary Vaynerchuk's work and be impressed. The craft, the intensity, the omnipresence, and the Hollywood-style production value are enough to get you high on motivation and beautifully crafted entertainment.

Yet, it can also leave you on the sidelines, because if that's the standard you're looking to achieve, it's going to be nearly impossible. Similarly, if you're a speaker and start comparing yourself to someone who's been in the game for 20 years and commands $50,000 for a keynote, you can lose your momentum easily.

Go back to that person's first iteration of whatever they are doing and dive into it. These days, in a virtual, on-demand-access world, it shouldn't be difficult to find. Spend some time looking at their early work, and you'll flip the switch. You'll be inspired by how far they've come—and how they once were in the same position you are in now, or even worse.

Gary Vaynerchuk's first YouTube video is a prime example—crappy graphics, a raw Gary, a bad haircut, and no keynote speech clips from thousands in the crowd. In your industry, you too can identify one person and go back to their start or early evolutions and, instead of letting yourself off the hook, become inspired by what's possible for you.

FALL IN LOVE WITH DELAYED GRATIFICATION

Instant gratification is an endurance killer. As a culture, it has become the expectation that you and I can have anything we want right here, right now, with very little work.

Want to go on a hot date tonight? No, you don't have to stir up the confidence to talk to her and risk rejection. You can swipe right.

Want to get in killer shape? No, you don't have to show up at the gym and risk looking awkward. Burn your fat off with laser treatment.

Want to have an amazing meal? No, you don't have to cook anything and learn a skill. Simply click a button and it's yours.

Sure, there are countless benefits you and I experience every day with the ease and availability of apps, smartphones, and the digital ecosphere. However, because this has become the status quo, we run from delayed gratification in nearly every life circumstance.

The easiest place to see this is our waistlines. As of print, 40% of adults and 19% of children in the United States are classified as obese. This is not an issue of know-how, access, or information. It's simple human behavior:

We're unwilling to delay gratification of our most basic human desires.

While I do have empathy and compassion for people who struggle with their weight, if you're unable to delay gratification with food, that's on *you.* Everyone knows what to eat, and access to healthy food is more affordable than ever. We can create a laundry list of excuses and circumstances to justify the choice of eating unhealthily, but the key word there is *choice.*

In order for you to endure, you'll inherently have to fall in love with delayed gratification. You'll have to put off the Friday night party so you can do the work required. You'll have to say "no" to trips and experiences you may want now that will get in the way of your vision. You'll have to sacrifice income and a steady paycheck to achieve the business of your dreams.

One of my mentors at one of the world's most grueling and intense physical training facilities, Gym Jones in Salt Lake City, once told me:

Everything costs something—and I mean, everything.

The lesson here is that there is the perception that a slip to instant gratification is no big deal. But it adds up when you add in time and the endurance factor.

ALWAYS MOVING FORWARD

In September 2014, I participated in a race called Spartan Ultra Beast, nearly 30 miles of physical and mental endurance hosted at the Spartan Championships in Killington, VT. If you've ever been there, you know Killington is known for its ski resorts and mountains.

The race course goes up, down, and around double-black-diamond trails. Every step of this journey was painful, and part of the course was designed to trick you mentally, with false mile markers and endless obstacle courses that bordered on torture.

I started incredibly strong. I tend to come out of the gates full force and not strategize my pacing. Halfway through the event, I was in the top 15% with some of the world's most elite adventure racers who do it full time.

However, I hit the physical wall, and I hit it *hard.* Being a well-rounded athlete means I can show up and finish nearly anything, but I was unprepared for the physical toll on my knees, hips, and calves from running on an incline for sixteen hours.

Every step was a dose of blistering pain, vibrating my hips all the way to the bone. Furthermore, my left leg and quad were unable to fully lock out. In the depths of this raging pain, I was reminded of a simple lesson a mentor once shared with me:

Focus on the next step—right here, right now.

In other words, it's easy to start feeling sorry for oneself and want to give in or to think how much further we have to go. I remember looking up at another double-black-diamond mountain trail and feeling so far away from the top. I'd done it seven times by now, and I knew how hard it would be. I saw people laying on their backs, grimacing in pure exhaustion—and I wanted to stop.

I kept moving, focusing on the present, and embracing the current step. On your path, and in your life and business, you too will experience these moments. As we mentioned earlier, Seth Godin details this in his brilliant book, *The Dip* (Godin 2007), where he identifies the dip as the point where you're starting to face the biggest hurdles and challenges, and you enter the process where endurance will be required.

This is where most people quit because it's *hard.* It's grueling. It's a double-black mountain when you can't lock your leg out and want to stop. It's another Friday evening alone at Starbucks because you're committed to shipping your content. It's when you can strum guitar chords, but your fingers scream in pain and you want to smash the guitar in your living room like Kurt Cobain because you're frustrated that you can't get it.

Yes, I've personally experienced all of those, and I know you can relate.

The ethos behind the 1% Rule means you're going to take at least one step today. Even if you're exhausted and on the verge of giving up—you take the step. If there's nothing else you do that day, tomorrow is a new chance and a new opportunity. However, each time you persist in the face of adversity, you build a confidence in yourself that you will execute and grow when the chaos hits, and this will serve you for the entire journey.

TAKE NOTE ALONG THE JOURNEY

I sat in the Buddhist meditation class and looked around. I noticed I was the youngest person there by at least two decades. As we went around the room, we introduced our reason for being there, our *why* behind taking a weekend off and spending time in deep meditation and spiritual study.

As I shared my piece, a man in his 60s turned around and told me:

"Son, embrace that you've chosen to be in this room at your age. I'm telling you, the fact you're here is unbelievable, and I wish I would have had the awareness to start when you did."

Seemingly simple, but this man will never know the deep impact this had on the rest of my life. From that moment on, I embraced all types of growth and experiential training in a way I hadn't before, because I could feel the regret in his eyes and voice.

Furthermore, it reminded me to appreciate every moment of the path. You and I are led to believe success and achievement are a Hollywood-style, music-blaring, fist-bumping dance party where smoke clears the room, and we're left with our prize. The reality is not nearly as dramatic and often we can be left disappointed by this illusion. What you and I will remember is the journey. In 2017, I gave a speech titled *The Journey Is the Win* at an entrepreneurial event in Phoenix where I hammered home the point.

In the midst of chaos and uncertainty, the last thing you want to hear is how beautiful the journey can be. However, it's what you're going to remember. Right now, as you read this, you're on your journey. While I don't know your exact evolution, I can tell you this with the utmost certainty:

One day, you're going to look back and reflect on this period of your life—and miss it. You're going to miss the excitement, the doubt, the beautiful mess of ambition and desire, the growth, the studying, the wins, and the losses. Sure, you will love your results and the life you've created, but don't miss out on the moment right now.

CULTIVATING ENDURANCE

Endurance is a mindset, a secret weapon that will serve you beyond your wildest dreams. The moment you become obsessed with the process and the consistency required for endurance, everything changes. You do the little things you don't want to do, decision-making becomes easy, and you fall in love with the 1% progress you're experiencing every single day.

Cultivating endurance is a choice and starts with one born out of commitment. In today's society everyone has high expectations. We've mentioned this several times. But they usually come with low commitment.

Let me explain this with a graphic:

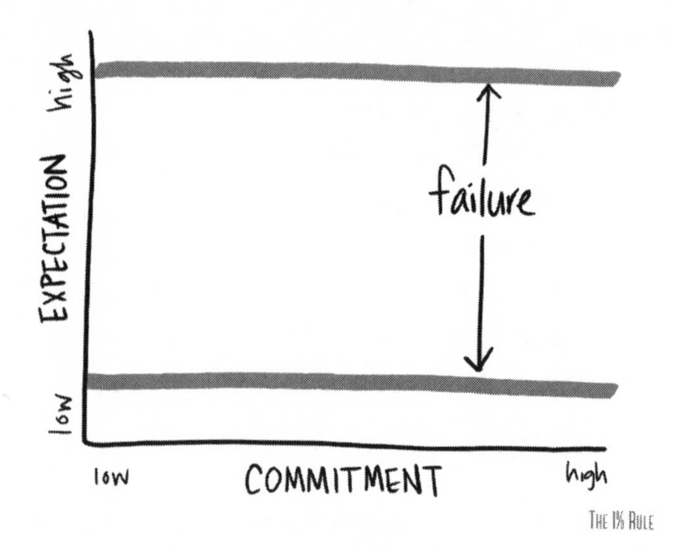

Here, the expectations are sky high—a thriving business, a functional body, a powerful marriage. However, once we look at reality, we notice the commitments are out of balance with the expectations. At this point, we have a choice:

Raise the level of commitments or lower the level of expectations.

If you're able to match your commitments to expectations, here's what it looks like:

Notice the difference? Those with high commitment are constantly cultivating the principles of the 1% Rule. We've already established it won't be easy, but it will be the most fulfilling path you'll ever experience. Below, you'll be able to identify your current level of commitment and expectations. You'll notice how identifying these and becoming honest about them will be liberating and refreshing at the same time.

As you go on about your own race, your life's journey, remember to stay in your lane. While watching others can give you a boost of inspiration, the real win is keeping your eyes on the daily prize as your successes start to add up, and the transformation that has evaded you comes to life.

YOUR TURN

It's time to receive your endurance score, by answering the questions below. Much like we've done throughout, it's crucial to be honest during this self-assessment and share with others.

1. What is my current level of expectations (what I want to accomplish in life) on a scale of 1–10?

   ____

2. What is my current level of commitment given those expectations on a scale of 1–10? Ask at least one other person what they perceive to be your commitment level. ________
3. Identify any gaps and choose one keystone behavior to bring your commitments in line with your expectations.

____

____

____

CHAPTER 8
The 1% Blueprint

1% PROGRESS + DAILY APPLICATION (CONSISTENCY) + PERSISTENCE (FOCUS) + TIME (ENDURANCE) = SUCCESS

We've gone deep into the power of the 1% Rule as a concept for life and business. We've discussed the importance of living by a set of principles, or a code. We've reviewed the back side of the equation: focus, persistence, and endurance.

Now we're going to break down the nuts and bolts of putting this into practice in your life. Note the word used: *practice.* That's exactly what the 1% Rule is. Practice means we're building, every single day. Much like a muscle, it's more about the tension we put on it consistently and less about the one time we lift enough to establish a personal record.

If the 1% Rule simply becomes another personal

development concept you never use, that's all it'll be. It will lie dormant inside of your head, jumbled with the 50,000 thoughts you're having, and not much will change. Maybe you'll see things differently, but we always revert back to our level of training, not our expectations. However, you can embrace the 1% Rule with everything you've got. You can center yourself to love the process and leave the illusions for others. You can make the daily choices and decisions born out of commitment and clarity, and everything will change.

In my life and the lives of countless clients, this change has happened. I've seen people afraid of heights launch themselves from 15,000 feet. I've seen people with no business plan or entrepreneurial experience create six-figure businesses in 90 days or less. I've seen people in marriages that were on the rocks have "the talk" and then keep the neighbors up all night with unseen levels of intimacy and passion. I've seen people do things they truly never thought were possible for themselves and walk into rooms differently.

You can be the next success story, but you've got to choose it. In a world telling you to choose others, remember your worth and *choose yourself.* It's your time because you're following the 1% Rule. We don't wait for the "right" time, the "perfect time" or when the economy gets better, or a new president enters the Oval Office. We don't wait for the holidays to be over, or for the calendar digit to turn from a 7 to an 8 to a 9 to get started.

We create the right time—in every single moment.

THE 1% QUESTION

Now that we've covered the core concepts, let's break down the 1% Rule in a practical manner. This concept is designed to be action oriented, and for you to start using it today or tomorrow, not in three weeks or three months.

One of the core tools of the 1% Rule is asking the right questions. Questions open up possibility in our minds and get us centered and focused. The 1% question is a tool in your daily arsenal to bring you back to center and correct course, or to identify what has to be done next:

"What can I execute on right now that will prove that my outcome and vision are not only possible, but coming true?"

> What can I execute on right now that will prove that my outcome and vision are not only possible, but coming true?

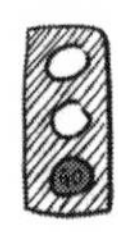

THE 1% RULE

Answering this question with intention will open up your world and give you clarity. It will keep you grounded and not in the clouds. It will engage your left and right brain to come up with a logical, yet creative solution. It will force you to focus less on the "how" and simply take the next step in front of you. It will keep you from the constant paralysis by analysis that has plagued you for years or even decades. It will strip you of distraction, fluff, gossip, and the urge to check Instagram for the 97th time today. It will put you in a place of knowing in a world of chaos.

Let's break this down step by step and see why it stacks the odds in your favor.

What can I execute on right now...

First, we're forced to identify *one thing* amidst nearly infinite possibilities that alone will get us hyper-clear. We then pair this insight with execution, getting us off the sidelines and taking a committed action. The amateur lives in a world of insights and "aha" moments and stops there. The pro uses these by being in the game and executing on them. Simple distinction, but transformational in the realities of your life.

... that will prove that my outcome and vision are not only possible, but coming true?

Here's the magic sauce, because it's one thing to identify what to execute on right now. Most people know that. They know it, but they don't follow through. Which is why we ask the powerful second half of the question, forcing you to connect the dots with your vision.

In this case, we're looking to ensure that your vision and outcome are not only possible, but coming true. This is crucial because, as we've said before, you and I are used to writing down goals and resolutions, going to big corporate planning retreats—and then doing nothing. The binder stays on the shelf, the book is half-open, and every time we pass by it, we feel a little guiltier and a little less compelled.

This question forces you to identify the action step necessary to make your vision come true. At the end of the day, there is no number of law-of-attraction meditations, inspirational social media quotes, dance-party seminars, or other forms of inspiration as powerful as the greatest motivational force on this planet:

Progress.

Or *perceived* progress.

As humans, we are natural inspectors. Whether we realize this consciously or not, we are always collecting data. If, after committing to a goal, outcome, or vision, we don't see progress or perceived progress, we'll quit. We won't last the marathon if we're not seeing the progress by mile seven. We won't achieve the business goal if we don't see some light at the end of the tunnel. Notice the words chosen: progress or *perceived* progress. It's enough to believe progress is around the corner and on its way. All that matters is we feel progress, as this will keep us going long enough to see the results we've been waiting for.

The 1% question becomes your artist brush and your answer becomes the brilliant masterpiece you're creating.

Whenever you experience chaos, are thrown off kilter, or are questioning your path, simply ask yourself the 1% Rule question.

"What can I execute on right now that will prove that my outcome and vision are not only possible, but coming true?"

Using this question on a daily basis will prove priceless to you—if used with intention and clarity after you've done the work required to know where you're going.

PARKINSON'S LAW

We're all crammers. Human nature dictates we are, so your tendency to cram for your final exams in high school and college has likely carried on well into adulthood. Many times, we won't even start until we can't go one second longer and we have our backs up against the wall.

Urgency in life *matters* but it must be used the right way, and without the constant rollercoaster we've all experienced. Parkinson's Law (Parkinson 1955) is one of the most studied, researched, and used concepts in productivity for great reason. The principle, written by C. Northcote Parkinson, is simple:

Work expands so as to fill the time available for its completion.

Here's how this looks in your daily reality:

You knew your best friend was getting married months in advance, yet waited until the last few weeks to hit the gym.

You submitted a proposal at work on Monday for the following week, yet didn't start until Friday night.

You commit to cleaning your entire place on a Sunday, yet don't start until it's time to go to bed.

We've all been there, and it can be outrageous how much we can get done at the last minute. However, this is not a long-term strategy for success. It's stressful and usually leaves us exhausted the next day.

What makes Parkinson's Law powerful is that it mirrors a universal law where empty space will be filled by the lowest possible priority. One of my mentors, Dr. John Demartini, taught me this in Houston, Texas, once when he said:

If you don't fill your day with high-priority items, others will fill your day with low-priority items.

The question is designed to help you break through and specifically identify the action step you're committed to achieving. Without the question, we are lost in a sea of chaos and distraction.

ANSWERING THE QUESTION

Asking the question isn't enough. We've become used to answering questions half-heartedly without the proper intention or specifics. In order for the 1% Rule question to really work for you, you'll have to dig deeper. We're masters at procrastination and rationalization. It's a super-sized muscle we've flexed too many times. Much like the guy who only trains his biceps, we're out of balance.

Naturally, you're going to experience resistance. Below, I'll touch on why resistance is actually something to look for. Without it, you wouldn't be growing and expanding. Answering the question must be done in an intentional way to produce the result we're looking for.

Here's how to unleash the power of asking yourself:

What can I execute on right now that will prove that my outcome and vision are not only possible, but coming true?

Be hyper-specific. Leave no detail out. Identify the most common denominator when answering this question. Your brain loves complexity since it allows for procrastination. What exactly are you committed to executing? Not nineteen things, not a massive plan that can be broken down over and over: choose *one* thing.

Be intentional. Intention matters. If you answer the question simply to answer the question, there'll be no deep-rooted *why* behind it and you'll lose focus. It isn't just showing up that's 80% of life, it's showing up with *intention.*

Connect to your vision. In the next chapter, we're going to ensure you have undeniable clarity around where you're headed, connecting the dots to your bigger vision. Without clarity on this vision, the little details become hard to execute.

Create a domino effect. As showcased in the brilliant book *The One Thing* (Keller and Papasan 2013), executing on the step you identify usually makes other things easier. That is why it is often called a keystone action. A keystone is simply the leverage point allowing for a cascade of momentum.

If the answer to your question contains these, you're on the right track. You're deliberate, and you will be rewarded with the gift of clarity and execution few others in the world have. Remember, this is new to you, and we've got to implant these habits in your daily reality, which means asking and answering this question every single day.

E-MAIL AND SOCIAL MEDIA CAN WAIT

If you answered the question with e-mail and social media, try again. Even if your position is a social media manager or professional e-mailer, you're going to answer it again.

E-mail and social media are clarity killers—and put you in the driver's seat for someone else's vision.

They're addicting and designed to be this way. According to Dr. Sriram Chellappan (Vishwanathan et al 2013), assistant professor of computer science at Missouri University of Science and Technology:

"About 5 to 10 percent of all Internet users appear to show web dependency, and brain imaging studies show that compulsive Internet use may induce changes in some brain reward pathways that are similar to that seen in drug addiction."

We've become a culture obsessed with checking e-mail all day, many times even working with the e-mail tab open, waiting to be distracted. The power of the 1% Rule comes in identifying the weekly and daily execution steps that truly move your life and business forward. Former President Dwight D. Eisenhower gave a speech in 1954 where he stated:

"I have two kinds of problems: the urgent and the important. The urgent are not important, and the important are never urgent."

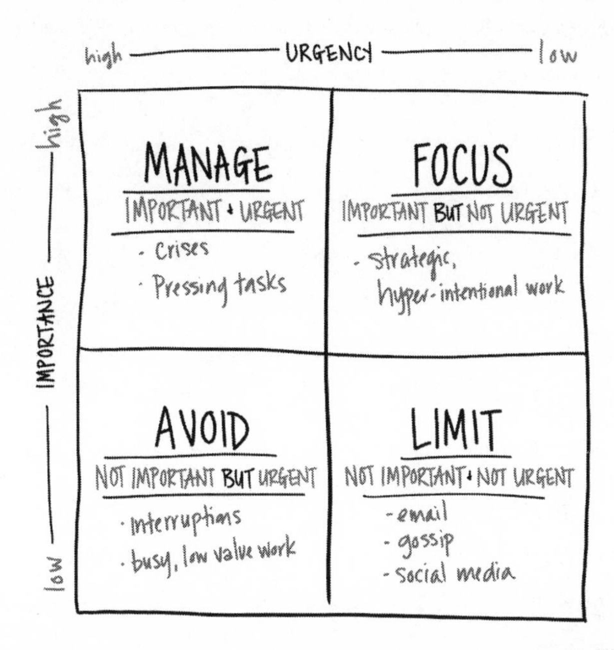

As shown in the chart above, most people live in the world of high importance/high urgency and high urgency/low importance. As a culture, we're *trained* to do the busy work that makes us feel productive yet doesn't truly move us forward.

Using Parkinson's Law, we quickly realize that today's "high urgency/high importance" happened because we were distracted and procrastinated the day before. The activity or execution step wasn't essential until we waited long enough to make it a pants-on-fire moment where we must get it done.

This is not a strategy—unless your goal is to live in a world of chaos.

Where are you spending most of your time? I know the answer, and so do you. You're likely addicted to the busy work, multi-tasking, e-mail, deadlines, shipping messages in and out, and being distracted through the process.

You get to the end of your work day, and you're feeling exhausted but proud that you've done tons of work. However, deep down, you know you were simply busy, not productive. It's a hollow feeling, especially if you work for yourself.

The 1% Rule and framework is going to shift your priorities by starting your day off with intention and purpose. Instead of starting out with high urgency/low importance or high urgency and importance, you're going to start out with an action step associated with what really moves the needle in your life and business.

As you begin to flex this muscle, you start shifting the tide. You'll go from being addicted to "busyness" to being addicted to focus and productivity with a level of momentum you've never experienced before.

AUDIT DELETION

In working with clients to achieve massive clarity and integrate their vision into daily reality, I've noticed a trend:

They're operating on a foundation that's ready to *implode* at any moment.

There is no space, and stacking new habits, rituals, responsibilities, and tasks on this foundation is bound for failure. As we mentioned earlier, capacity and bandwidth are crucial in life yet extremely limited. Where most consultants and coaches go wrong is adding before deleting, then wondering why their clients simply can't execute and follow through.

For the 1% Rule to truly work, you're going to have to create space in your life. This requires you to take inventory, or do an *audit*, and delete what's not serving you. Once you've done this, you can strategically insert what's aligned with your vision—and things become simple.

Specifically, you're going to conduct an audit on the people, places, and environments that currently surround your experience. We're going to delete the ones that aren't serving you. Brendon Burchard, *New York Times* best-selling author of several books, including *High Performance*

Habits (Burchard 2017), works with high-end corporate clients to the tune of $250,000 a year. The first place they start is *deletion*—looking at this individual's calendar and creating space. If it's good enough for them, it's good enough for you.

Right now, over 50% of what is in your life is not serving your vision. You've allowed relationships to stay around because they're comfortable—you grew up together or went to the same college. You visit environments that used to serve you but now hold you back. In the context of business, you're doing countless tasks yet 20% of them drive 80% of your income, impact, and results.

This isn't a wild guess, it's science. Every time you level up and achieve a new breakthrough, audit your circle. Every time you grow and expand into a new experience, audit your surroundings. Every time you hit a new business goal or outcome, audit the information you're consuming.

Every time you level up, audit your circle and environment.

The more you can delete, the more room you have for production, creativity, and real *thinking*. Yes, in a microwave world, thinking is a superpower. Your mental real estate is priceless, and if someone is staying up there, they better pay for it. However, we let people into our minds rent-free, and never serve an eviction notice. Your real estate is not a run-down home in the slums—it's beachfront property. It's of incredible value, and everyone wants it. It can't be quantified in terms of dollars—it's priceless.

Let's start recognizing this and deleting what doesn't serve.

RESISTANCE

On your quest to incorporate the 1% Rule and answer the daily question, you're going to experience *resistance.* Resistance is simply the voices inside your head telling you not to do it. Resistance is the fear-driven, comfort-zone-loving version of yourself that identifies with the current you. Change those circumstances, create a new reality, and it freaks out, bringing you back down. It's in love with the *known* and sees the unknown as a threat.

Resistance is responsible for killing countless dreams and passions. It's responsible for half-written books, unfinished vision boards, and depleted spirit and energy. It's what you feel when you wake up on a Tuesday morning on little sleep, and don't want to get out of bed. It's what you feel long after the high of starting has worn off. It's all-encompassing, all-consuming, and will crush us unless we understand it and learn to love it.

Stephen Pressfield, the brilliant author, describes why resistance is a prerequisite, not an obstacle, in his book *The War of Art* (Pressfield 2012):

> "Resistance is experienced as fear; the degree of fear equates to the strength of Resistance. Therefore, the more fear we feel about a specific enterprise, the more certain we can be that that enterprise is important to us and to the growth of our soul. That's why we feel so much Resistance. If it meant nothing to us, there'd be no Resistance."

This is where the reframe occurs. When you experience resistance, laugh at it. Smile at it. See it for what it is—a sign you're growing. It's much easier to live in a world of distraction, as we've said earlier in the book. By facing resistance, you build a fortitude and grounded confidence in yourself that you can't acquire, sell, or buy in twelve payments of $9.97.

Undoubtedly, I will get the question:

What do I do when everything tells me not to follow through and not get 1% better today?

The answer is one most people don't want to hear, but it's the truth:

Lean in, and double down. Learn to love the resistance and understand the courage it takes to live a life on your terms.

DAILY GAME

While our commitment is serious, don't take everything in life too seriously. When diving deep into the 1% Rule and resistance, the moment you discharge the power of what you're doing with laughter and humor, you win. No longer will it hold this mystical power over you. You'll be able to execute on command and turn it into a game.

For me, writing this book has become a daily game. This is being written in a season of my life where I've never had so much happening at once. So instead of taking myself so seriously, I have fun and let go.

I step into a playful attitude around this work, and it eases and soothes the pressure. The truth is I don't want to write every single morning at 4:00 a.m. Yet, here I am. Darkness surrounds me, except for a few burning candles and the screen staring back at me.

I'm having the time of my life.

Your goals are serious; they're life or death. We're much closer to the end, than the beginning, and it can all be over in a moment. However, there is a beautiful dance or paradox where we marry the seriousness of our goals and outcomes with the lightheartedness of humor, play, and fun.

Trust me, I've learned this the hard way. I always operated out of blunt force, and I was rigid. However, there is no magic in being rigid. As we dive deep in the next chapter on vision, clarity is of crucial importance, but so is being *open* to what's possible. And in order to be open, we have to be in an abundant state, or we'll miss it.

When I work with a new client, I only care about one thing: their level of openness. If they're coming to me, it means there's a problem. However, if they're not open, we will never be able to create the results they're looking for.

Let's bring this concept of being open down from the clouds for a moment. Think about the last time you were stressed out to the gills—overwhelmed, scattered, and running on fumes. Maybe it was earlier this morning or a week ago.

In that moment, were you *open* to opportunity? If you had come across something magical—a person, place, environment, business idea, connection—would you have seen it? The answer is *no*. You wouldn't have seen it because you were so rigid, stiff, and tight in your awareness that you only thought about yourself and what wasn't working.

This is exactly what we want to avoid. Otherwise, we'll miss the secret sauce that takes the 1% Rule from simply a concept of incremental growth, to an ethos and principle of deep-rooted fulfillment and magic.

YOUR TURN

It's time to practice. No matter when you're reading this, answer the question.

"What can I execute on right now that will prove that my outcome and vision are not only possible, but coming true?"

Decide what I should write about
____

____

____

____

CHAPTER 9

Craft Your Vision

I was *nervous.* I was at an intense event, and I had a sinking feeling in my gut I would be called on. I'd had plenty of time to come up with an answer, yet that was working against me.

That's when he turned to me, held space, and asked, "Why are you here?" as he pierced me with his eyes on a cloudy California morning.

I answered what sounded nice yet wasn't deep in my heart. *Try again, that's not what you really want.* Breathe, I thought to myself, then I spit out my second answer. *No, not good enough, that's not what you really want. You're lying to sound good.*

Crap.

I was startled and didn't know what to say or do. During the next 45 minutes, I would be challenged, pushed, supported, and revealed in front of others so I could achieve clarity on where I wanted to go with my life. It included what I thought was possible for me, and we didn't stop until I had tears running down my face.

Without a vision for our lives, you and I will perish. We will perish in confusion, doubt, uncertainty, and the daily chaos of bills, taxes, titles, roles, and more. What I detail in the story above is true about your vision, too. We have to peel back the layers and get you to a place where you're giving yourself permission to think bold and big. We have to ensure it's deeply important to you and hits your emotional heartstrings. We have to ensure we've let go of the beliefs that are already stopping us from getting there, including the *how.*

What differentiates the 1% Rule from other similar concepts is the rest of this book. We're going to take the concept through a process I call *The Integration Experience*—a way to connect the dots between the massive visions you and I have in life and bring them down to today. During the last few years of in-the-trenches coaching and consulting, the most common thing I heard was:

> *Tommy, I've read the books, I've listened to the shows, I've even gone to the seminars. I get excited, I get hyped*

up, yet never create anything that lasts. The empowering information starts to become disempowering because of my lack of results. I lose faith, I don't trust the process, and I can't seem to get out of my own way. I question if everyone in this industry is simply lying, and I can't do it. I want to turn this information into results.

Sound familiar? We've all experienced this. It's time to break through this cycle and get clear on every part of making your dreams, aspirations, and goals come to life—using the power of the 1% Rule.

LET GO

I want you to let go. No, truly, I want you to let go. I want you to let go of what has happened today as you read this. The issues, the conflicts, the opportunities, and the moments of doubt. I want you to let go of what's happened this week—the struggles, the laughs, the smiles, and the frustrations. I want you to let go of what has transpired this entire year. No matter what has happened, I want you to let it go. Let go of the moments of doubt, let go of the stress around all the moving parts of your life and the roles you play. Let go of the uncertainty and fear of the future and the current struggle you're in right now. I want you to let go of what's happened in your entire life leading up to right now. Take a trip down memory lane—the good, the bad, and the ugly. The moments of despair and sadness, and the moments of incredible joy and tears of gratitude.

Today, I give you permission to let go of it all.

We begin, once again, with deletion. We create the space to allow you the bandwidth and capacity to think bigger and bolder. Right now, I can feel your resistance.

I've heard this before.
Please, not another vision exercise.
Last time I did this, nothing happened, and I felt worse.

Without this resistance, nothing would matter. The resistance is exactly what you need to know there's a gift within this exercise, and you're being triggered. We start by letting go to create new space and step into a new version of yourself. Your foundation is already too heavy—too many tasks, too much responsibility, and way too much on your plate.

Before you move on, ensure you've let go. Otherwise, none of this will work.

PAINT YOUR MASTERPIECE

You have a blank canvas on your hands, and you've got the brush and the paint ready. No matter how many times you've done this in the past with little to no success, it does not matter anymore. Without a vision, or what I call a *North Star* guiding you through the daily chaos, you'll be lost.

If I were to grab people walking by on the street and ask them their vision, I'd get generic, pie-in-the-sky answers that sound like perfectly scripted Hallmark cards. Many times, it's not even what they want. The guiding compass in your life becomes your vision, and must specifically include the following three components before moving on:

I: Massive Clarity

It's a broken record by now, for good reason. Without clarity, life becomes confusing and decision-making is impossible. Your vision must be crystal clear. You'll work on it through the rest of this chapter. It's not enough to have an idea or a sense of where you're headed. You need to take yourself to the place, drop your current reality, and step into a new one. The moment you can detail a day in your future life with everything you've created and accomplished, down to the seemingly insignificant moments, you've achieved clarity.

II: Big and Bold

This is no time to play small. Unlocking your possibility requires you to give yourself permission. Yes, only you can honor yourself to think bold and big. If it makes you uncomfortable, fantastic. Your vision *should* make you uncomfortable, otherwise it's corporate, incremental, and vanilla. Do not get lost in the "how." Focus deeply on the most inspiring "what" you can imagine. Only to the bold will the world yield. Speaking your vision should make your voice tremble in excitement, nervousness and passion, all mixed together like a summer cocktail.

III: Emotionally Charged

At the end of the exercise, if you've done the above and communicated your vision, it must pull on your heart. If you don't get emotional through the process, start over. Your vision is not created out of logic and reasoning, it comes from deep within. It comes from a place much bigger than your head—your heart, your spirit, your all-encompassing, all-knowing life force. With that said, you must be able to tap into your *why* in a way that brings tears to your eyes. In working with clients, we stay here until they do. Otherwise, it's not deeply important to them and they haven't connected the urgency of this experience deeply enough.

NORTH STAR

Celestial navigation was the only way countless ancient civilizations knew where they were. Using 57 navigational stars, sun, or moons, our ancestors were able to navigate the world, find new lands, and ensure a guiding compass.

None is more guiding than Polaris—the North Star. Fixed in the northern sky, the North Star is easy to find and marks the north celestial pole.

Your vision, then, becomes the guiding light to help you understand where you are and where you're headed. In the book *Finding Your Own North Star* (Beck 2002), Martha Beck details it brilliantly:

> *"No one but you has the ability to find your own North Star and no one but you has the power to keep you from finding it. No one."*

Once we've identified our North Star and our vision, we've achieved clarity. We're not going to focus on the *how* yet—that's coming. What identifying our North Star does is ground us in the here and the now and eliminate the cloudiness. The topic of vision is discussed endlessly, yet most people do it wrong. Because of this, they have little proof it will come true, and they lose their momentum.

Worse off, they stop believing it's possible for them. It's very likely you rolled your eyes at this chapter and thought to yourself, "Not another vision exercise." As we discussed above, embrace this resistance because it means there's a part of you that hasn't fully bought in. We'll talk about how to ensure you do this time.

TEST DRIVING

Let's imagine you identified your dream car and knew the exact make, model and color. You headed to the dealership to check it out, and there it was in all its glory.

You stepped into it and felt different, so you decided to take it for a spin. The car's feel, aesthetic, and power exceeded your expectations. You handed the keys back to the dealer and left without purchasing it, but it stayed imprinted in your mind.

As you left the dealership on that day, you started to notice that the car you had just driven, felt, and touched was now everywhere. You saw it on the highway, parked at your local grocery store, and everywhere in between. You'd see it out of the corner of your eye, or even sense it before it came to your awareness.

We've all experienced this, and it's the power of a focused awareness. The same sort of thing will occur with your vision. Once you've stepped into it—observed it, touched it, smelled it, felt what it would be like to have that reality every day—you operate differently.

You walk and talk differently, and your energy shifts. Furthermore, much like you saw the car everywhere, you start to notice things you didn't notice in the past. You notice people, places, and environments designed to assist you toward your vision. People come out of the woodwork, strangers naturally are drawn to you, and you start to feel a deep sense of alignment and certainty. A teacher or mentor appears at the right place and right time. You listen to a snippet of a YouTube video that startles you in how specifically it connects to your vision. You receive a random message from a random stranger on a random day—and then recognize nothing in life is random.

Here's the truth: all of this was available to you all along, you simply didn't *see* it. It's not that you physically couldn't see it. It was there, waiting for you to make a decision. It was waiting for you to make a choice. It was waiting for you to get clear. It was waiting for you to have the courage. It was waiting for you to commit. It was waiting for you to open your heart and mind about what's possible for you and believe it with every fiber of your being.

With this clarity, everything changes.

ARIZONA

Nearly three years ago, I had a moment of intense clarity: I needed to shift my environment or else I'd go on a route that wasn't for me. I was being pulled energetically over and over again. Living on the East Coast in Connecticut and New York, I started being pulled out West.

I craved space and knew within my heart something greater than myself wanted me to shift my physical location. I fought it with logic and reason, yet it persisted. I told myself it didn't make sense, but it kept coming. Finally, I had a moment I detailed in *UnResolution* where I made a commitment on a New Year's Eve night standing on an icy cold football field.

I didn't know how. I didn't know when. But I committed. I committed to moving to a place where I didn't know a soul, and to step into it in a year. The next day, I changed my smartphone background to a deep purple Arizona sunset with a cactus. I printed out a picture of a sunset and put it inside my car.

From that day on, my awareness shifted in a way I'd never imagined. I'd go into float tanks and meditations and see the blistering sun in Arizona. I'd open up a magazine and see an advertisement for Arizona tourism. Every day I'd meet someone and they'd mention Scottsdale or Sedona—and it was no mistake.

What had occurred was simple.

My focus of awareness was intensely set on this new vision, and anyone or anything designed to help get me there faster started to appear.

Within six months, I found myself at McDowell Mountain, a nature preserve in Scottsdale. As I hiked down the mountain during a beautiful sunset, I looked up in awe. The exact sunset I had set as my smartphone background—the same deep purple sky, the same type of cactus, the summer haze—was in front of me.

This moment brought tears of gratitude to my eyes. I had completed my vision in less than six months. This required massive changes before I could follow through, including the selling and dissolving of a business I'd only recently signed a five-year lease on.

THE TIGHT ROPE

The power of crafting your vision is *undeniable* and will absolutely empower your life. However, there is a powerful principle I must share about this practice to ensure your success and deep levels of fulfillment along the way.

Even though I want you to be as detailed and vividly intense as humanly possible when you set your vision, it is crucial to not be too rigid, or else you may miss out on something that could light your world on fire, but that you don't have the perspective to see.

This is the dance, the tightrope of a vivid vision combined with the infinite possibility of life. Along the journey, there is no doubt your clarity will serve you.

It will keep you grounded.
It will keep you connected.
It will keep you focused.

However, on that journey, opportunities will come up. Opportunities you can't imagine right now because of your vantage point. You think you know, but you have no idea. Since life is not linear, or predictable, you'll be presented with opportunities or paths that will open up your world in ways you could have never imagined.

This is where the magic happens—on the tightrope. It's the powerful combination of focus and awareness, intensity and openness, clarity and possibility. The reason this will serve you is simple:

If you stay open to possibility, you may find an alternative vision that you currently can't imagine and will absolutely blow you away.

SURRENDER

Surrender. Not quite the word you'd imagine in this book, yet an absolutely crucial concept. Surrender completes the two sides of the tightrope:

The intensity and focus of your vision with surrender to the potential possibilities.

This dichotomy is deeply rooted in spiritual texts and will serve you. We've all met those people who try to control everything around them. Maybe that person is us.

We are stressed, anxious, as we attempt to influence and control others. We end up disappointed because we can't control anyone except ourselves. The greatest way to influence is not directly—it is by becoming a beacon and allowing others the space to do to the same.

Attempting to control others for the sake of our freedom is a fruitless endeavor. This is where surrender comes in. Surrender does not mean giving up or giving in—it's quite the opposite. Surrender means being "all in" to a point where you let go of the clenching grip you have on life and open up to the depths of what can happen.

Once you've set your vision, reaffirm it every single day—we'll go into the practices later in the book—and be relentless in your execution of this grounded clarity, while surrendering to what may be possible for you. In interviewing and examining countless titans of industry and other greats, I found that their initial visions were meager compared to where they ended up.

They could have never imagined what was possible for them, but they completely gave into the process and woke up one day in a place that seems like a dream.

CRAFTING YOUR VISION

It's time—your time. I urge you to complete this section in a place where you're truly able to open your mind, create space, and be in a powerful state. In doing this exercise with countless people, I've seen that the stress of our lives or our current emotional state can zap all the energy and intention out.

You'll find a guided meditation in the resources section to ensure your success and your clarity through the process. As I mentioned above, right now is the time to let go. If you stay stuck in the past or in what hasn't happened yet or in how your high school girlfriend or boyfriend broke up with you, it won't work.

Inhale, exhale—and let it all go. I want you to center yourself to right here and right now. With every breath, I want you to begin to let go of what's happened today and be in the moment. Start by noticing. Notice yourself and your body relative to space, and your place in it. Go within and listen to your heartbeat pumping relentlessly, as it has for the decades you've been on this planet. Shift from what hasn't happened or what is stressing you out to complete and utter gratitude. Now, I want you to take yourself to a place. This place is magical—serene, beautiful, full of life. You are surrounded by nature and the sun shines down on you. There's a mountaintop with the most beautiful sunset you've ever seen, and the first star of the night has come out. Out of the corner of your eye, you notice a door in the middle of this mecca, and it is calling you toward it. On the other side of this door is the vision for your life. Specifically, on the other side of this door is your one-year vision.

When you step through this door with all your clarity, energy, and abundance, there is magic waiting for you. It's the most beautiful, bold, and empowering door you've ever seen. As you step closer to it, your heart starts pounding a little stronger, and you feel the presence and power on the other side. There's even a little fear at the vast energy it's giving you, but it's a grounded fear you know is designed for you, and you're embracing it. As you step closer, you take one last breath and open the door. On the other side, you feel a sense of deep and authentic gratitude. Tears start flowing down your face in awe—you've accomplished more in the last year than the decade prior. Your heart, mind, and body are full, and you can't believe what you're seeing. You look around and go through a day in your life on this side of the door and the depth of fulfillment and what you've achieved is extraordinary. Go through your day with a deep level of awareness. Really see it. Paint a picture in your mind of what it looks like. What do you wake up to? What is your environment? Who is there with you? How do you start your day? Go through each step of your day and see the people, places, and environments that have been created from this powerful intention and have supported you and your vision through the last year. As you do, you stop yourself for a moment and realize you had it all along, you were worthy, and nothing was missing. You smile back to the frustration, the stress and the anxiety you can now see wasn't serving you. You feel deeply grounded and excited for this experience. You easily and effortlessly attract unbelievable opportunities and synchronicity through your experience. As you look around and experience this reality, I want you to take notice of your health, your vitality, how you feel that day. I want you to notice what your purpose, meaning, and income are, to the last cent. I want you to notice how connected you are to others, but also to yourself. I want you to notice the relationships in your life and how much depth you now have with them, and how deeply connected you are. I want you to paint me a picture in crystal-clear detail and leave nothing out.

At this moment, I hand you a pen and paper and ask you a simple question:

What did you see in your vision? Write it down now, leaving no detail out.

____

____

____

____

BELIEF IS THE SECRET SAUCE

As you come back from the exercise, you'll know if you did it the right way. You'll feel it. If you have any doubts, go back into it. If you experienced any type of resistance in regard to this exercise, that's great. As we've identified previously in the book, resistance is truly a gift and signifies you must lean in further to discover a lesson, or a new perspective to help you going forward.

Once you can tell me with intense vividness where you're going and what's calling you, everything will change and shift in your life. Yes, the 1% Rule is built around making progress every single day, but it has to be connected to something bold and powerful. Otherwise, you won't want to continue when the challenges and doubts arise. You'll lose the power of the vision you created.

Regardless of the journey you took through the exercise, your level of belief in what you painted will ultimately dictate your success. One of the crucial mistakes I've noticed with those who use or teach this vision exercise, is looking at belief as a one-time deal.

Belief is cultivated, it is exercised. Much like a muscle, it can grow or contract every single day.

> Belief is cultivated - much like a muscle, it can grow or contract.

THE 1% RULE

Reaffirming this vision every single day becomes your weapon and allows you to increase your belief and flex the muscle underneath. In the resources section, you'll find a simple daily vision exercise and meditation designed to bring your vision back to life and center you in seven minutes or less.

YOUR TURN

Complete the vision exercise at least once and use the daily vision exercise to reaffirm it at least once a day. Ensure you have gone through the checklist below.

Did I let go before starting my vision? [Yes/No]

____

Did I allow myself to think big and bold? [Yes/No]

____

Did I truly believe what I painted is possible? [Yes/No]

____

Did my vision bring me to tears of gratitude? [Yes/No]

____

Once you've answered yes to all of these, you've secured a powerful vision destined to help change the game for you. If you answered no, you'll need to spend more time with the above. Now it's time to make this vision a reality using the tested and proven principles of the 1% Rule.

CHAPTER 10
Reverse Engineer Your Success

The gap.

You know *the gap*—the one between where you are right now and the vision you detailed with crystal-clear clarity. This gap, this void or glaring chasm is where dreams, aspirations, and visions go to die. It's why people stop doing it altogether, because they feel worse, not better, about themselves. It's the space between, the "how," the endless paralysis by analysis.

The gap can be your catalyst or your anchor. Ultimately, it's your choice. Within this chapter, we're going to help you make it your catalyst and show you how to use it as a way to supercharge what we've already done up to this point. Without this, nothing matters because you won't follow through.

If you skipped the prior section, go back and complete it. In order to close the gap, and use it as fuel, we're going to need to have you extremely clear, focused, and intentional. In consulting clients, the *gap* is the issue that comes up time and time again.

Not anymore. It's time to tackle it head on and set yourself up for extreme success.

SCREW THE HOW

"But...I don't know *how* I'm going to close the gap, Tommy. My head is already spinning, and I'm already stressed...and we haven't even started!"

Ahhhh, the common response after we've set the vision. We go from being high off the possibility to depressed about the logistics. Without a doubt, the "how" is the gap's favorite weapon of mass procrastination and, ultimately, destruction, **designed to keep you swirling in a world of confusion until you give up.**

You're letting the *how* win—and ultimately stop you in your tracks. I can't tell you how many times I've been knee-deep in a consulting session when I've seen my client's eyes wander toward the *how*. Their body language, vitality, and energy completely shifts—and they start to believe a little less.

The *how* is where dreams go to die.

If left to their own devices, they'd be crushed by this. Luckily, I'm there and able to identify this clearly, because I've been the person on the other side trying to figure out the *how* too.

The reverse-engineering process we're about to take on is going to replace your *how*, but for now, I want you to tell the "how" part of you to get out. For too long, this part of you has derailed you, distracted you, and created chaos and uncertainty in your life.

The *how* is solely responsible for:

Crushing your dreams after you get a brilliant insight from a seminar.

Stopping you cold in paralysis by analysis after you make a powerful decision.

Helping you live your life on the sidelines, instead of on the field of play.

Derailing you the moment you choose to talk to him or her and making you play small instead.

Worst of all, the *how* expands when you feed it what it really loves: *time.*

The more time you spend analyzing, dissecting, or thinking about the *how*, the less likely it is that your goals, outcomes, and vision will come to fruition. This chapter, then becomes your secret weapon to pulverize the *how* mindset once and for all.

WHAT WOULD HAVE TO HAPPEN?

Now that we've gotten that out of the way, it's time to take a step back. Once you've set your vision, I want you to exhale. Literally. Release the doubts, the fears, and the insecurities and simply take a moment. As I write this, I am literally visualizing myself putting my vision on a whiteboard, like I've done for myself and my clients, and physically stepping back.

Stepping back allows you to digest your vision and takes the pressure off. It allows you to connect the dots and examine the varying aspects of what you're looking to create. Many times, it brings an extra dose of clarity and even confidence as you tell yourself:

"That's not only possible, I can truly make this happen."

It's a powerful moment rooted in perspective. Once you've taken a step back, you've created a little more space for you, which will serve you the rest of the way.

Now we're going to answer a simple yet powerful question in your pursuit of bringing this vision to life.

In order for you to feel your vision is not only possible but coming true at a faster pace than you even imagined:

What would have to happen in the next 90 days?

This is where we take our one-year vision—which can be powerful and overwhelming at the same time—and bring it down to ground level. I want you to paint a picture of yourself waking up in 90 days and noticing real-world proof of your vision coming true.

What exactly has changed in that moment?
What are the tangible differences and results?
What are the intangible differences and results?

Answer these questions and keep them close as we continue to move through this chapter and the exercises.

IDENTIFY YOUR BIG ROCKS

Now that we've created some space and taken a step back, it's time to identify your big rocks. When I say big rocks, I mean the pillars you'd need to have in 90 days to prove to yourself that everything was coming true, that would give you confidence that you have the momentum to make it happen.

Let's face it:

There's no number of Instagram quotes or YouTube videos that can get you as motivated and inspired as the proof of your vision coming true.

As we mentioned earlier, progress, even perceived, is extremely powerful for your continued thrust to action.

When identifying your big rocks, we must ensure the following:

They're proving your vision coming true. Connecting the dots here is crucial. Ensure your big rocks can be easily connected to the vision we set earlier.

They're realistic, yet you get nervous with them. If you don't feel some butterflies in your stomach, they're not going to stretch you. Remember—fear and nervousness are required in this case.

They force you to execute on a high level. You're nervous because these big rocks will force you to spend most of your time executing and less time on the sidelines thinking and analyzing.

They truly matter to you. Again, they must matter to one person: *you*. If you're doing these for someone else's approval or recognition, you'll give up long before the finish line.

BIG ROCK BREAKDOWN

For your big rocks, we're going to break it down to ensure your success in the core pillars of your life.

The four pillars will include your Business & Purpose, Health & Fitness, Spirituality, and Relationships.

For each of the four pillars, we will:

Identify core outcome. The core outcome is the end result you're looking to achieve for that pillar in life during the next 90 days. It is deeply connected to the vision you set earlier.

Identify core process. Every outcome has a process associated with it that is the keystone action step designed to ensure the outcome is a success, or has a high probability of achievement and follow-through.

Identify 1% process. We further break down the core process using the 1% Rule—a measurable, daily way of moving forward. This is designed to simplify the game and give you clarity every day.

Below, we'll look at examples for the four pillars of life.

BUSINESS & PURPOSE

CORE OUTCOME: My core outcome is to generate $35,000 during the next 90 days.

CORE PROCESS: My core process is reaching out to 2,500 leads during the next 90 days.

THE 1% PROCESS: My 1% process is to generate 27 prospect calls every single day.

HEALTH/FITNESS

CORE OUTCOME: My core outcome is to complete the Spartan Beast in 90 days.

CORE PROCESS: My core process is three gym workouts a week and two long hikes.

THE 1% PROCESS: My 1% process is daily activity and hitting my nutritional requirements 85% of the time.

SPIRITUALITY

CORE OUTCOME: My core outcome is to create more inner peace and reduce the stress in my life.

CORE PROCESS: My core process is to wake up 15 minutes earlier to allow the time.

THE 1% PROCESS: My 1% process is a daily meditation for a minimum of 7 minutes.

RELATIONSHIPS

CORE OUTCOME: My core outcome is strengthening the connection in my marriage in the next 90 days.

CORE PROCESS: My core process is creating six date-night experiences and one big-trip experience.

THE 1% PROCESS: My 1% process is to encourage my partner with creative appreciation every day.

These big rock examples are designed to help you get clear and drill down on the outcome, the process, and the 1% process. With this process, there is no room left for uncertainty. Instead, there are deep levels of clarity as we continue to apply the 1% Rule to your dreams and outcomes.

Before moving on, you're going to take the time to identify each of your big rocks, including the Core Outcome, Core Process, and 1% Process. Do this now before reading further, or else you'll forget or miss a crucial part of the experience.

Now, to be clear, you will need to do more tasks than only the 1% process. However, the purpose of this process is to identify the nonnegotiable focus you must have every day *before* moving on to the other tasks.

Think of it this way: the 1% process is designed to be the straightest path to your outcome. Many times, it can also be the most difficult, and the one where you experience more resistance—which is a great thing. We identify and tackle these first, as they not only pave the straightest path to our outcome, they create a domino effect where the rest of the work becomes easier.

Then, we build our days around this process, and stack in the other objectives, which we'll detail below.

WEEKLY ROCKS AND TASK DUMP

We're making progress, baby. I feel it, you feel it—everyone feels it. (Cue scene from *Old School* where Will Ferrell's character says, "Everybody's doing it.")

Now that we have our big rocks, we're in a great place and gaining more momentum. Next up, we're going to go through a powerful process of creating bandwidth—increasing your ability to step into your big rocks with focus and clarity. For each of your big rocks, you're going to make a list of everything that you believe needs to be done to complete the outcome. Don't overthink it—simply write them down.

Using the Business/Purpose outcome, here's what that looks like:

CORE OUTCOME: My core outcome is to generate $35,000 during the next 90 days.

The initiatives, steps, and tasks associated with the above are:

» Hire PT admin

» Launch referral campaign

» Increase prices

- » Create auto-responder
- » Schedule a client appreciation day
- » Ask for referrals
- » Continue over-delivering and fulfilling
- » Create calendar for prospect calls
- » Schedule sales calls
- » Make prospecting a priority
- » Obtain new leads from company
- » Set up new website

NOTE: *Again, we have already identified the 1% Process, but we now make a list of everything else we believe will be associated with this objective during the next 90 days.*

Don't move on to the next step until you have the smallest of tasks figured out.

Step 1: Deletion

Look at everything you wrote down and delete what doesn't serve your big rock. There's always a handful of activities we simply need to delete, and here's your chance.

Step 2: Automation

Identify which things on your list can be automated. What are you doing right now that can be done using software or systems?

Step 3: Delegation

What initiatives, tasks, or projects are important yet can be delegated? Whether or not you have a team, we now have 5 billion people online. Finding cheap resources to clear things off your plate is easy. Identify what can be delegated right now.

Step 4: Weekly Rocks

If you've done the above correctly, you should be left with the core essentials. This is the high-level, zone-of-genius type work only you can do. If that's not the case and you still have fluff here, go back through Steps 1, 2, and 3 one more time. Now you're going to look at what's left and rank them in order of importance, with 1 being the highest, and 3 being the lowest. Work your way down. You may have multiple 1s, and that's totally fine.

Now that you've achieved this rare clarity, we'll continue the process of reverse engineering your success, leaving no details out. You'll never be the same after executing and seeing the magic of this process.

BIG ROCKS TO 12 WEEKS

At this point, you should be feeling clear and inspired. You should know what you want and why you want it. You should know how to measure your success and what you have to do every day to make it a reality. Congratulations, you now have massive clarity. Not only do you have clarity, you have certainty—the certainty of how to get there. You no longer have to sit on the sidelines waiting, pondering, or analyzing.

In other words, you've got a game plan. You've got a strategic blueprint to close the gap, maybe for the first time in your life. Don't take this lightly. It's a huge deal and if you've done all the exercises to this point, **you're in the 2% of people who live an intentional life.**

These big rocks will be your guiding force for the next 12 weeks, or 90 days. We work in 90-day increments because it's enough time to accomplish an incredible amount of results, yet short enough to provide high levels of urgency.

Once you've identified the big rocks, your vision will fade into the background. No, you won't forget about it—there are tools designed for you to reaffirm your vision daily. But you'll bring your big rocks into what we call "sniper level focus," ensuring your follow-through happens every single day.

Remember: you don't have to hit a home run every single day—you simply have to get in the game.

Whether you hit a single, get walked, or steal a base, what matters is you're in the game and growing. If you go one for five, that's perfect—and should be celebrated.

Little hinges swing *big* doors, and all your efforts will pay off—but you've got to stay consistent. Now that we have your big rocks, we're going to create your first week of targets. Separating the 90 days into 12 weeks allows us to bring our focus down to a closer level—the 6 inches in front of our faces.

For example, let's take the big rock from before in business:

BUSINESS & PURPOSE

CORE OUTCOME: My core outcome is to generate $35,000 during the next 90 days.

CORE PROCESS: My core process is reaching out to 2,500 leads during the next 90 days.

THE 1% PROCESS: My 1% process is to generate 27 prospect calls every single day.

Now you're going to create your weekly blueprint to ensure your success. Given the core outcome, the core process, and the daily 1% process, here's what you're going to do:

When planning out your week, identify the three or four key action steps that must be done in order for you to connect the dots and prove that this week you got closer to your Core Outcome. These will come directly from the list we created in the prior section, what remained after you deleted, automated, and delegated.

Here's an example:

Week 1 Blueprint

Action Step #1: Complete 27 prospect calls daily, or 138 for the week.

Action Step #2: Launch referral campaign to current clients.

Action Step #3: Hire part time admin to help with tasks/client work.

You're off to the races. We don't do all twelve weeks at once because if you use the tools of focused intensity in this book, you'll blow past what you thought was possible. Additionally, overplanning can lead to distraction, as we've mentioned, and we're here to keep you focused and on fire. If you do this right, you would have completed at least 36 core actions in your business each quarter, leading to transformational results. At the end of this week, you'll reflect, pivot, and chart a new course using the above as you move toward your target every single day and week.

12 WEEKS TO 1% EVERY DAY

Now that we've been able to simplify the entire game for you, we bring it down to today. This system was created after years of getting hyped up about visions and outcomes, yet not knowing exactly what had to be done on a day-to-day basis.

Let's face it:

Anyone can get hyped up and excited at a dance-party seminar and create an epic vision. The real question is what do you do with that on a cold and rainy Tuesday morning, when you're tired and had a fight with your partner the night before?

That's real life, and why we bring it down to the 1% level. Otherwise, the dopamine hit of visualizing our outcomes will be simply that, another source of entertainment and temporary feel-good chemicals.

Not here, because your goals and vision truly matter to you.

THE DAILY QUESTION

When you wake up in the morning through your 90-day experience with the big rocks, review your vision from the top, all the way down. This may take you 30 minutes or 3. What matters is the level of your intention behind it, not the duration. After you've reviewed your vision, you ask yourself the question we revealed in chapter 8:

What can I execute on right now that will prove that my outcome and vision are not only possible, but coming true?

Answer the question and then do nothing else until you've executed. Don't check e-mail, do not text, do not wait. Every second you wait is an opportunity lost, the loosening of the grip of momentum, which you can't afford.

This is your life, and if you care enough about what you've committed to in the prior chapters, you'll prioritize it and minimize distractions and chaos. Sure, in 2018, that's easier said than done, but we're not here for easy. We're here for you, because *you* matter.

If you've made it this far, you should be experiencing a feeling you haven't in a while, if ever. We've closed the gap for you and instead of it being a place where dreams go to die, it's where your dreams will now flourish.

It'll be where you find the deepest sense of fulfillment and achievement, and you'll never look back. It's the place where you find an inner confidence you've never experienced before, and step into certainty and conviction. It's the place where you have a deeper sense of knowing that making your dreams a reality is only a matter of time.

You're here.

Now it's time to bulletproof what we've done, creating a system of ruthless execution on your quest to bring your vision to right here, right now.

YOUR TURN

Before moving on, ensure you've gone through each step of the reverse-engineering process. Be deliberate and focused and do it twice, if needed.

CHAPTER 11

The Roadblocks

1% PROGRESS + DAILY APPLICATION (CONSISTENCY) + PERSISTENCE (FOCUS) + TIME (ENDURANCE) = SUCCESS.

The 1% Rule is a formula, a proven and tested way to create the life of your dreams by growing ever so slightly every single day. It's for the tenacious few who understand and embrace that the process of growth is never linear and requires the pillars of focus, persistence, and endurance to stand the test of time.

You're reading this for a reason—you want more out of life. Whether you're in a dark place and need to get out or you are already successful and want to continue to level up, it's all the same. If you use the 1% Rule, the daily question, and the reverse-engineering process we just went through, your life will never be the same.

In this chapter, I'm going to discuss some of the traps

or pitfalls that can stop you in your tracks. I share these because they are all too common and will divert you off the path we've outlined. Becoming aware of these now will help you, since it's not a matter of if, but when they come up.

IT'S TOO SIMPLE.

It can't be this simple.

I've heard this countless times—and I always smile. For years, I ran athletic performance training facilities and every single time I'd create a training session and someone said, "Wow, that looks so simple," they'd find out it was the hardest session they'd ever done.

What's simple is powerful, although never easy.

In life, we should all be chasing simple. Anything else is noise and distraction, something we have way too much of these days. When people believe something is too simple, they're afraid of what comes next: *the work.*

If things are complex and require endless planning, blueprints, and meetings, then we can avoid the work today and put if off until tomorrow, next week, or next quarter. This is why companies will spend millions of dollars on strategic retreats and create beautiful binders which end up sitting on the shelf. It's why the solopreneur focuses on small, insignificant tasks. It's why we constantly feel we need a little more time and planning.

No, thanks. Simplicity is the name of the game and I encourage you to lean into it. The more you can simplify and streamline your processes down to answering the 1% Rule question, the more you'll create the unbreakable momentum designed to push you over the edge.

BUT I WANT BIGGER RESULTS.

But I want bigger results.

The idea that we can have big results with low commitment is one of the big delusions in today's society. Everyone has become a convenient critic, and from the sidelines it is easy to believe we could have done better.

For example, when the wide receiver drops the crucial pass on third and nine, it's easy to say:

"I would've caught that."

But nothing could be further from the truth.

Because your vantage point, your perspective, is sitting on

a comfortable couch on a Sunday, three beers and a few nacho platters in.

In other words, you're not in the game. You're not feeling the pressure, intensity, the crowd, the high-stakes environment that athlete has spent an entire lifetime training for. You're not feeling the silent footsteps of a thrashing 6'2", 246-pound linebacker who is about to jackknife your body in half.

Most importantly, you haven't been a part of the process, including the countless sacrifices, decisions, moments of frustration and doubt, and all the practice, reps, and enduring consistency of pursuing a dream.

The truth is:

You wouldn't have caught that pass, because you wouldn't even be in the game. And so, in life, it's easy to look at someone else's success and say:

"I could do that, too. That's easy."

You see a thriving business or an app that's blowing up or a best-selling author, and it looks easy. But it's not. Much like the receiver, you're only seeing a snapshot of the story.

And it's not that you *can't* do it, because you're certainly capable. You simply haven't put in the reps. You haven't taken the risks they have, doubled down on yourself, put all the chips on the table over and over and over. You haven't experienced the sleepless nights, the pressure, and the intensity that comes with what they're doing. And so, the lesson is simple:

If you want the big results and your own third-and-nine opportunity, double down on the process and work behind what you've put to paper. It's not as easy as you think or else everyone would be in the game with an opportunity to get the first down.

Commit to the work and watch what happens. One day, you'll be in the game—and someone will tell you how easy it looks, and how they're going to do the same. You'll smile, knowing you once thought the same.

THEY'RE CRUSHING IT.

They're crushing it—and it's making me feel worse.

Let's face it: it is human nature to compare ourselves to others. Especially if we're on a path of growth, we become hyper-aware of what others are doing in a highlight-driven world. I love when authors and speakers simply tell us not to compare ourselves to others, because it's bullshit.

It will happen. Accept this reality. When you and I compare ourselves to others, we have two choices.

The first option:

Stay stuck, let ourselves off the hook, and be disempowered. It's easy to see someone else's success and think, "Well, if they're so far along, why even bother?" We see their success as unattainable and create a narrative around why we're not good enough or capable of getting that far. This is the status quo of comparison and it manifests in the following symptoms: paralysis by analysis, hopelessness, starting and stopping, and ultimately giving up.

If that doesn't sound good, you have the second option:

See their success as your own greatness being reflected back to you. The moment you recognize someone else's success and greatness as a reflection of what you're capable of, everything changes. You're inspired by them, and you're compelled to believe in yourself more deeply. You fall in love with the possibility—they're the real-life proof you can do the same.

You and I don't know everyone's story. They may be crushing it, or they may be in a world of hurt. We all have much more depth than we show the external world, and your perspective will either serve you or won't. If you want to remind yourself of the power of *starting*, simply identify the people you most admire and go back to the first iteration of what they've created.

Read their first book, listen to their first podcast, watch their first acting role. You'll quickly notice they once started somewhere too—and they had the audacity to keep going even when they weren't anywhere near as skilled as they are today. They believed in the process, celebrated it, and continued to improve 1% every single day until incremental progress turned to exponential results.

I'M IN PAIN

I'm in a lot of pain.

When people come to me and express their pain, I tell them to celebrate it. It sounds crazy and wild, but I remind them of a powerful distinction:

Your pain is your power and contains a gift. Sure, this sounds great on paper, but in the midst of chaos it's the last thing you want to hear. You simply want your pain to be fixed, soothed, and healed. I get it.

Here's why your pain is a source of power: it centers you and helps you focus on what truly is important today. It brings you down to the right here, right now and eliminates distractions. We've all experienced this: a brutal workout, a tough hike, a relationship conflict, a painful injury, the moment we get called by HR to the boardroom and we're fired. In all of these examples, we become centered and fully present in the now.

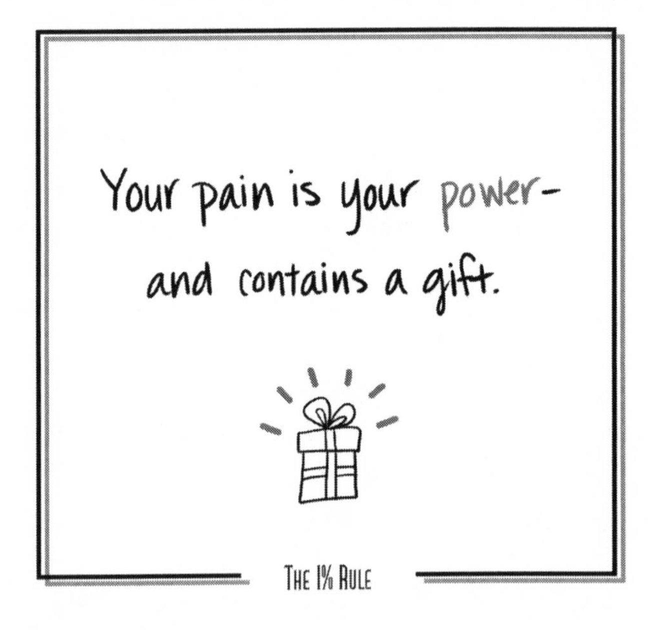

In that place, we make powerful and bold decisions. The moment I was fired from my first corporate gig, I made a committed decision to start my fitness business. The moment I endured a painful breakup where my partner was unfaithful, I made a committed decision to work on myself in ways I'd never done before. The moment I experienced a rare, debilitating lung condition and was on my deathbed, I made a decision to reinvest in my health. You've had countless of these moments too, and while they are no doubt difficult, there's light at the end of the tunnel.

Right now, you may be in that state too, and I want to encourage you to make a committed decision *now.* Not tomorrow, but this very moment. If the pain weren't readily available, you may not have the audacity to make that decision. You may be "good enough" or living in the land of "maybes" where dreams go to die.

THIS SEEMS BORING.

This seems boring.

Highlight reels are sexy, the real thing isn't. If it seems boring to make 1% progress every single day, you're right. However, the alternative is to create sky-high expectations, get hyped up on dopamine, launch your nineteenth business—and never move the needle forward.

I'll take boring results over pie-in-the-sky fantasies any day of the week. The truth is, no matter how excited and on fire you may be with your visions and outcomes, there are going to be long periods of boredom within them.

Being in a rock band seems pretty exciting, right? Until you're on your eleventh straight night in a random hotel room in Omaha, Nebraska, and have to do yet another sound check.

Being an actor or actress for a feature film seems amazing, right? Until it's 11:30 p.m. and you started make-up at 4:45 a.m., and you're bleeding out your eyeballs after doing the seventeenth take on the same exact scene and your supporting actors can't get it right.

Being a best-selling author sounds pretty fun, right? Until you've written an entire book over the span of two years, then threw it out and started from scratch, and now you're experiencing an existential crisis.

Boring is part of the process—embrace it. If you believe you're going to be hyped up on passion and dopamine 24/7, you're playing the wrong game. Warren Buffet, the world's most celebrated investor, is known for having a pretty boring life and investing philosophy. Yet, at the same time, it's impossible to argue with his success.

Yahoo Finance (Ryniec 2017) said this about his style:

"If Buffett's 'formula' could be described in a word, that word would be 'boring.' Wonderfully, profitably, enjoyably boring."

IT'S NOT THE RIGHT TIME.

It's not the right time.

Even after a 55-minute conversation where they left no detail out about how much pain they were enduring, they say, "It's not the right time." Earlier in the conversation, this individual had told me how they knew they needed to stop living in fear and stop only using logic. They needed to make bold decisions:

Steve, you've just identified how your lack of decision-making and living in fear is holding you back. Now, when presented an opportunity to create from a new place, you're telling me it's not the right time. Do you see a pattern here?

Talking ourselves out of our dreams simply because of the season of life we're in or because of a calendar digit is a bulletproof way to get and stay stuck. As I've mentioned earlier, perfect timing is an illusion. It lets us off the hook, so we don't have to summon the courage to make a decision and execute it.

The right time is created by the power of a bold decision.

The word *decision* means to cut off, to slice off what is no longer serving and move forward with clarity. The timing will never be right. Even if you can argue that today is a bad time because it's the holidays and you're on overdrive at work, it won't get better in February. Then you'll have a new issue replacing the old one and the vicious cycle will repeat itself.

Create the right time in your life and you'll never look back.

I CAN'T FIGURE OUT THE HOW

I can't figure out how I'm going to do that.

As we mentioned earlier, the *how* is the graveyard to your dreams—where they go to die, buried once and for all. The *how* is where people stay stuck in a never-ending loop of research and analysis and an inability to execute. Without a doubt, if there's one place where we lose our initial excitement and enthusiasm over anything, it's here.

I always smile when people go from the unlimited potential of their vision to the graveyard of the *how*. You can sense it in their voice and body language, their belief slowly self-destructing one moment at a time. The truth is, you don't need to figure out the *how*, at least not yet.

The *how* is not some grand plan, a blueprint, or a treasure map, it's the resistance showing up in full force. If you did have every step of your vision laid out, it wouldn't be yours. Or worse, it'd mean you were playing safe and small because we could easily identify every tiny step on the way to the peak of your mountain.

Remember:

When the *what* and *why* are bold and vivid, the *how* starts to reveal itself.

It starts to reveal itself step by step. But you've got to have the audacity and courage to take those first few steps. Instead of figuring out every step of the *how*, commit to one or two steps. Execute with blinders on. Stay consistent, and then rinse and repeat. Use the 1% Rule to begin to carve out your path, and you'll notice the *how* becomes obvious. You'll realize it at the time, but also know you could have never seen it when you were starting out—because you didn't need to see it.

WHAT WILL THEY THINK?

What will they think?

Here's the truth: no matter what you do in this game of

life, you will be judged. It's part of the human experience, and we can't delete it from our reality.

But if your dreams and vision are hinging on one person's viewpoint, then you're done. It doesn't matter how close or far away this person is, you're not thinking bold and big enough. Many times, people will stop cold in their tracks because of what someone might say.

If you will be judged regardless of what you do, you might as well play full tilt.

I love entering conversations with people who are consumed by what others are going to think or say about them, because quickly we realize the resistance comes from the fear of validating their own internal critic. This is why external noise and critics affect us on a deep level, and can even stop us cold.

It's not about them—it's about what they're saying that we've already told ourselves.

"You're a crappy writer."
"This message is too much."
"No one's going to listen."

Once you realize this, you can smile and detach through the entire process. There are so many people online wasting their time and energy talking shit about others when they could be using this energy for powerful creation.

Remember: if you lower your intensity and ambition to please a certain few, you'll miss out on attracting the tribe that wants you to play all out.

It's a Catch-22, and you'll wind up pleasing the silent critics while resenting yourself every single morning when you wake up. If I stopped every time I was labeled, or a stranger left a comment on a video, this book wouldn't be in your hands right now. At some point, you have to let go. Ultimately, you will get to a place where the praise and criticism don't move the needle for you. You simply continue to ship your message because it comes from the heart, and that's all that matters. The right people will be open and listening, even if you never hear from them.

Whenever I get too caught up in my own head about what others are thinking, I'm reminded of a famous quote by author David Foster Wallace from his book, *Infinite Jest:*

"You will become way less concerned with what other people think of you when you realize how seldom they do."

The truth is, everyone else is too busy thinking about the same thing you are: what others will think. This, then, liberates you to detach from what others think and care about what one person really thinks: yourself.

YOUR EXCUSES ARE NO LONGER VALID

We've gone through the major resistance roadblocks you are bound to experience, and they're now gone. However, you and I are masters at creating more excuses and somehow talking ourselves into them. These will come up time and time again and on a daily basis.

Furthermore, as you do grow, expand, and accomplish, they'll come back stronger and in different forms.

Don't let this sidetrack you; it's part of the journey. From this point on, you're going to be so ruthlessly focused, they'll pass by you. You'll even start to appreciate them as feedback mechanisms and proof you are growing and headed down the right path.

This chapter could have been another 100 pages. I could have filled it up with all the excuses available to you and me on a daily basis, many we've used in the past and continue to use today. They're all the same, and the source is equal across all of them: resistance.

CHAPTER 12

Urgency & Accountability

As we've said, there's no perfect timing—your time is now. If you keep waiting to get started, you'll wake up one day and wonder what happened—and where it all went.

Most people act as if they'll have all the time in the world later on, a technique to let themselves off the hook. However, you and I know life won't get less busy or complex. And as we've mentioned several times, the "perfect" timing is simply a choice.

Now we're going to cover some secret weapons to help you rise above and execute on the highest of levels. The reality is, our experience here is nearly over. No matter how old you are, the clock is ticking, and every day is a reminder. Every birthday and New Year's creates a reflection period where we ask how far we've come, and if we're really living.

This is where urgency and accountability come in. Creating urgency in life is crucial to cutting out all possible distractions and narrowing down on all the work we've created together so far. It's about creating some space between the stimuli and getting real.

Here's what these two look like working together:

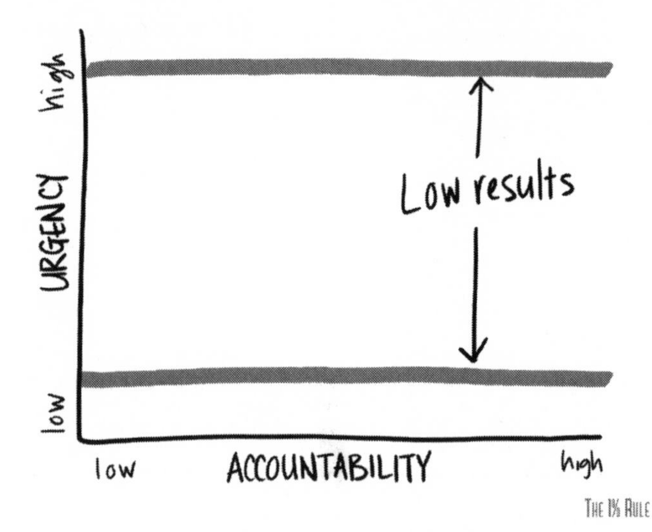

Alternatively, when you combine high accountability with high levels of urgency, here's what you get:

You're here for results, plain and simple. During this chapter, we're going to break down the recipe to create your masterpiece and ensure your success every step of the way.

ON THE SHORTNESS OF LIFE

Two thousand years ago, a Roman stoic philosopher named Seneca the Younger wrote a text, *On the Shortness of Life* (Corpus Scriptum Latinorum 2017). In the text, written as a letter, he beautifully articulates the predicament you and I currently find ourselves in. Amazing how, even then— without the stimulus and endless distractions you and I face—culture was still embedded in distraction and sedation.

This text has become required reading for all my programs, for good reason. If you're able to truly sink your teeth into it, it can be an uncomfortable read. The reason is simple: Seneca lets loose on how most of us live our lives—concerned by everyone's opinion of us, wasting time, and dreaming up big plans with nothing to show for it.

> "You live as if you were destined to live forever, no thought of your frailty ever enters your head, of how much time has already gone by, you take no heed. You squander time as if you drew from a full and abundant supply, though all the while that day which you bestow on some person or thing is perhaps your last."

This overarching urgency is a beautiful reminder to have in the back of our minds. We are so consumed by the day to day—the tasks, the bills, the responsibilities, what he or she did or didn't say, breaking news, clickbait, and sports radio—it's a wonder anyone stays focused long enough to create.

The reminder that our lives are short and death is near is empowering. The vision and outcomes you've set in prior chapters are not to be taken lightly. You've gone through the process and invested your time and energy—don't let yourself off the hook.

The truth is, your vision is a matter of life or death and should be respected and treated as such. If you're truly here to create a masterpiece with this experience, this reminder will keep you going when you're not feeling like it.

It'll help you take the much-needed next step every day to begin bringing all your dreams into reality.

CREATING INSPIRATION

What separates the pro from the amateur in life is simple:

The amateur sits around waiting to be inspired while the pro creates inspiration.

> The amateur sits around waiting to be inspired—while the pro creates inspiration.
>
> THE 1% RULE

Creation runs deep within our DNA and is an essential part of who we are. Which is why creating in life feels amazing and fuels us, regardless of how you create—having a deep conversation, running an event, playing an instrument, or shipping a marketing message. It ignites a deeper part of you designed to express the unique creator inside us all.

All of the feelings most people wait for to get started or get serious—inspiration, energy, zest, passion, purpose, excitement, intensity, desire, fulfillment, abundance—are on the other side of stepping into the unknown and taking action.

Waiting for these seems like a great idea at the time because it lets us off the hook, so we can sit back on the couch, hang out, and be entertained. Not here. You're a *creator* and it's time to create those feelings. Through your journey, there are going to be plenty of moments where you'd much rather sit on the couch and wait. What you do with these micro-moments will ultimately determine your success.

Last year, I was diagnosed with a rare and serious disease found in the dry areas of the country called Valley Fever. A regional disease, few people knew how severe it could be, and I spent weeks on my deathbed, trying to figure out what was happening. I was told I would never be the same again, and that this rare lung disease was an energy killer. Former Navy SEALs and pro baseball players who had it had retired due to the symptoms.

As I worked through the challenge, I barely had enough energy to shower on some days. Yet as the days and weeks went by, I started to do one thing every morning, one purposeful activity to start the day. The important thing isn't *what* I did, but rather just that I did it. I kept it small, almost laughably so. Yet I started to notice an uptick in my energy, ever so slightly. This is when I was reminded that you and I are here for something, and that deeper reason is what gives us purpose, meaning, and life-force energy.

As time went on, I started to include more of this purpose-driven time and my energy showed. One particular day, I was having an incredibly tough time and had coughed up some blood after an intense bout. That day, I had a podcast recording scheduled with Jesse Elder, an entrepreneur and consultant. Despite my poor health, I showed up. As I entered the conversation and engaged in something I absolutely love—deep conversations with powerful people—I forgot about my condition.

At the end of the conversation, it seemed a few minutes had passed when it had been over an hour, and the uptick in my personal energy was palpable. I left more inspired, grounded, and focused, even though the state of my health couldn't have gotten any worse.

Mind you, I didn't simply have cold symptoms. I was in the thick of a nasty disease. This is an extreme example of inspiration being *created.* And through your persistence to move your life forward at least 1% daily, you'll experience the same result.

MANUFACTURED URGENCY

Understanding that our life experience is short and will be gone in a moment is powerful, yet can easily be forgotten as you approach your day to day. While reading a classic text or reminding ourselves we don't have much time can push us slightly over the edge, urgency must be *manufactured.*

John Kotter, author of *A Sense of Urgency* (Kotter 2008) and professor of leadership at the Harvard Business School, explains how urgency is not natural, and can easily be forgotten:

"Urgency is not the natural state of affairs. It has to be created and recreated."

If we don't manufacture a sense of urgency, we won't move the needle toward consistent action and execution on a regular basis. This is precisely why we create 90-day cycles—enough time to create magical results, yet close enough that we're forced to execute.

Here are some other ways to manufacture urgency on the regular, and reap the rewards:

Cut your micro-target completion times in half. Intensity is jet fuel for creating urgency, and Parkinson's

Law will ensure you take the entire time. Instead, cut all your target completion dates in half, and get started now.

Set daily targets, and celebrate crushing them. Using the 1% Rule, set daily targets low enough to ensure success yet high enough to force you to push past resistance. For example, in writing this book I set out for 1,000 words a day. Once I'd gotten to 1,000, I usually didn't want to stop.

Declare your outcomes, and put yourself on the line. Declaring your outcomes to others will hold you accountable long after the high has worn off. Be careful how this is done—research shows that declaring your outcomes on social media may give your brain the same rewards as completing it and then halt your action. Instead, be deliberate about who you share it with, and put yourself on the line.

MASTERY AND ACCOUNTABILITY

As you grow, expand, and experience success, you'll need more urgency, not less. Complacency is an urgency killer and so is a little bit of success. It's the voice in your head that tells you to take your foot off the gas, and you know, "enjoy life a little more."

Make no mistake: this is resistance, this is fear. It's a

master at creatively stopping you in your tracks. Many people believe once they experience a certain level of success, or they accomplish their outcome, they don't need to continue to use the same level of urgency and accountability.

The opposite couldn't be more true. **The more you succeed and grow, the more urgency must be manufactured with higher and higher levels of accountability.** We've all experienced the back-up-against-the-wall mentality that forces us to produce and create at high levels. Then we get comfortable and let it all slide.

This rollercoaster wreaks havoc on our momentum and must be eradicated. When you grow and accomplish big outcomes, you tend to believe what got you there won't be as crucial as you move forward. Then begins the slippery slide back to mediocrity we've all experienced.

A professional football player is a brilliant example. The closer to mastery they get, the more coaches, intensity, accountability, and urgency is part of their game. As you climb up an organization, you realize the person with the most accountability is the CEO: they are accountable to their executive team, employees, and shareholders.

You'll need to do the same on your path and consistently

level up your urgency. When we add ruthless accountability to the mix, you'll never be the same.

RUTHLESS ACCOUNTABILITY

Creating a foundation of ruthless accountability—systems, people, and structures to ensure you follow through—will guarantee consistent production over the long term. I call it *ruthless* because it's not for the faint of heart and takes a high level of commitment.

Accountability is what makes everything tick and, without it, you and I are lost in the sauce. Much like urgency, accountability must be strategic and holistic in nature.

Here's why most people don't operate with high levels of accountability in life:

Accountability is inherently uncomfortable. We've put ourselves on the line, and now everyone knows it. Furthermore, we're operating under the agreement we're going to be called out, and that doesn't always feel great.

Everyone wants accountability until they get punched in the face with it. It sounds great on paper, or reading these words, but when you've had five hours of sleep and you're being challenged about why you didn't complete the crucial execution step you said you would, you aren't going to like it.

This is the inherent power of accountability: it compels us to action, gets us clear and honest, and manufactures intense levels of urgency. In the rest of this chapter, we'll explore why this is so crucial, what most people get wrong with accountability, and how to maximize it in your life to create the dream results you've been waiting for.

YOUR BUDDY GROUP WON'T WORK

One afternoon I spoke with an individual interested in my coaching and consulting programs. He seemed like a good fit, so I extended an invitation to him.

"Everything seems amazing, and I know I'd create next-level results. But I recently started an accountability group with some friends from work, and I don't want to be overwhelmed."

I said, "Got it. So let me ask you some questions to ensure your success with the group."

I then asked:

Do these people have the results you're looking to achieve in your life, both tangible and intangible?

Do these people challenge and push you to new levels of execution and intensity?

Are you bought in and invested physically, mentally, emotionally, and financially?

Who is running this group and who is the main leader who structures the programs? What are their results?

He didn't have many answers. These people didn't have the results they wanted, had never challenged him in the past, included zero investment and, oh yeah, they were leading the group and were in a world of uncertainty.

While he had amazing intentions, they were missing the core components of creating intense and ruthless levels of accountability. Mind you, the above could work for someone, but I'd call it a unicorn, rather than the norm. What I've seen in all my years is that, while creating the above sounds like a great idea, people lose interest after a few weeks because they're lacking the core infrastructure that makes accountability truly work.

ACCOUNTABILITY PILLARS

As I mentioned above, accountability is uncomfortable. Everyone wants it when they're feeling high, but when you're in the thick of things, you want to run away from it. This is precisely why you and I need heavy doses of accountability, because more often than not, we *won't* feel like following through on our outcomes.

With that said, there are pillars of accountability designed to ensure your success—and take you to places you've never been before.

Accountability is the reason you show up at the gym at 5:00 a.m. when every voice in your mind is telling you to sleep in.

Accountability is the reason you finish the last 200 words after an exhausting day, because you committed to finishing your book.

Accountability is why you hire the crucial team member in four weeks and not four months, because you're reporting back to someone daily.

Accountability is jet fuel for your results and requires the following four pillars.

Pillar #1: Four-Tiered Investment

In order for accountability to work, you must be invested. Anything in which we aren't invested won't be valued on a long enough timeline to produce massive results. Accountability requires the following forms of investment:

Physical. You're required to report back to someone by physically showing up. This may be in person or virtual, it doesn't matter.

Mental. A mental investment simply means your mental bandwidth and energy are purposefully used in the game of accountability.

Emotional. There's a deeply-rooted, powerful *why*, and your daily emotions are mixed into the game.

Financial. You've put your financial resources on the line because when you pay for things in life, you end up paying attention.

If you're missing one of these, your accountability system is doomed to fail. This four-tiered investment is required for your success and daily commitment to your outcomes. No matter who you are or what you do, you will not be inspired and motivated every single day.

Pillar #2: High Levels of Challenge

Accountability comes in many shapes and sizes, including mentorship, coaching, events, masterminding, consulting, and everything in between. However, a core and common theme among all of them is a healthy dose of challenge. As we've mentioned earlier, growth happens at the intersection of support and challenge, and without challenge, we slide into complacency.

Within challenge, we find out who we really are and embrace the power of consistent creation, always moving forward. Often in life, we surround ourselves with enablers who don't respect us enough to challenge us. It's the buddy who adds gasoline to the fire by supporting your complaints about your boss. It's the person who complains about being out of shape, and then goes with their coworker to Taco Bell.

Enablers in your life don't move the needle. You don't need them. If someone really respects and appreciates you and can see past the excuses you create, that's a powerful relationship.

Pillar #3: Powerful Perspective

There's a reason business consulting is a multibillion-dollar industry—*perspective.* Without perspective in life, we'd miss the blind spots we all have. If you've ever had a discussion with a friend, spouse, or coworker who was going through some challenges, you probably helped them achieve perspective. Since you were not in the trenches of their life, it was probably clear to you what they needed to do.

This clarity is nearly impossible to create in our own lives, regardless of how self-aware we may be. Accountability helps provide new perspectives, and new perspectives bring massive clarity. Without perspective, it's easy to spin our wheels and wonder why we can't get out of a rut or experience the breakthrough we've wanted.

With these pillars in place, you now have the ideal situation for success: high levels of urgency—both real and manufactured—plus a high level of accountability. This is the sweet spot where dreams come to life. This is where consistent execution is the name of the game, and we can compress one year's worth of work and production into one quarter or less.

MENTORSHIP & COACHING

"When the student is ready—the teacher appears."

Mentorship and coaching are some of the most powerful resources to help you create exponential results in life and stick with the concepts of the 1% Rule long enough to see success. Having a guiding light who believes in your potential and gives you the wisdom and perspective you need to carry out your dreams is invaluable and will pay off time and time again.

Coaching and mentorship help provide ruthless levels of clarity, direction, and accountability to supercharge results. They allow us to step into places we'd never imagined and take risks with someone who's done it before. It's a powerful and beautiful relationship built on trust.

Mentors and coaches come in all shapes and sizes. They can last for a day or for a lifetime. What matters is not the duration of the relationship, but the impact. One of my original mentors, Dr. John Demartini, speaker, consultant, and author once said:

"It takes one message on one day to change one life."

There are moments in our lives where we're required to take a leap. We know what we have to do, but we're lacking the courage. The leap into the unknown is difficult, and we'd rather stick to what's known and comfortable, even if it's challenging and there's pain involved. Without a doubt, I wouldn't be writing this book had I not had powerful mentors and coaches who allowed me to unlock the greatness within and learn to trust myself.

This is what a powerful coaching relationship does. Now that I'm on the other side and coaching and consulting with so many, it's become even more apparent. The role of a coach or mentor is not to do the work for you or to save you. As a coach, my responsibility is as follows:

I'm here to help you unlock the greatness already within you, the one you've forgotten about, ignored, or run away from.

Operating under this ethical duty is powerful, and there are many ways to get there. In most cases in life and business, we know what to do. If we could get rid of the fear and the paralysis by analysis, we'd be able to identify exactly what the next step or leap may be.

A coach or mentor becomes the safety net, allowing us to make powerful, committed decisions, even when we're surrounded by fear, chaos, and uncertainty. They become the beacon for us, the shining light that puts us in positions where we finally trust ourselves enough to follow through and do what we said we would.

LIFE & DEATH

If your vision truly matters to you, you'll create the systems and structures of accountability and urgency in your life to ensure it comes to fruition. Deep down, you know it's possible for you, yet the lack of urgency keeps you from fully committing, burning the boats, and going all in.

If it was a matter of life or death, you'd be all in. Here's the truth, however: it is a matter of life or death. Our time here is limited and will be over soon. Don't allow distractions or the illusion you'll be here forever let you off the hook. Remind yourself it's almost over.

This is not a negative mindset, it's quite the opposite. Living in reality is empowering because every moment counts. As Dan Millman, author of seventeen books, including *Way of the Peaceful Warrior* (Millman 2006), and Academy podcast guest once said:

"There are no ordinary moments."

This moment, and the next, are the defining moments in life. Don't let time fool you. Go all in on what you truly want. Express yourself, be creative, tell someone what needs to be said. This may be your last chance. Don't die with your song inside of you, unheard by the world. You deserve it, and they need to hear it. It's a matter of life or death.

YOUR TURN

Examine your life right now and take inventory. First, take inventory of the level of urgency in your life, on a scale of 1–10, where 1 is apathetic with zero urgency, and 10 is extreme levels of urgency. Then, identify one way you can increase it today, before moving on.

Now, take inventory of the level of accountability in your life. Who is truly holding you accountable, and at what level? Does it meet the standards and pillars we've described above? Rate it on a scale of 1–10 and identify one way you can increase it today.

My current level of urgency, from 1-10 is:

____

Here's one way I can increase it:

____

My current level of accountability, from 1-10 is:

____

Here's one way I can increase it:

____

CHAPTER 13

Putting It All Together

You've got the rule, the concept, the code, and the key pillars in place to maximize the 1% Rule. In other words, you're ready to launch. The time to consume is over—it's time to create. This becomes the beautiful process of going from knowing, to doing, to being. Every time you flex this muscle, you start to become the principles we've outlined, and they become your standard operating procedure in life. They change the way you see the world, communicate with yourself, and even how you walk into a room.

This powerful process allows you to use your incredible bandwidth on the creative process and thinking bolder and bigger. In this chapter, we're going to discuss the other side of the production and creation coin—the art and science of disconnecting and creating space.

If we don't create space in life, we lose out on some of the most valuable and life-changing perspectives available to us. This book wouldn't be complete if I didn't include this. In a fast-paced world, reflection is as important as action.

Let me rephrase that:

Reflection is as important as *intentional* action.

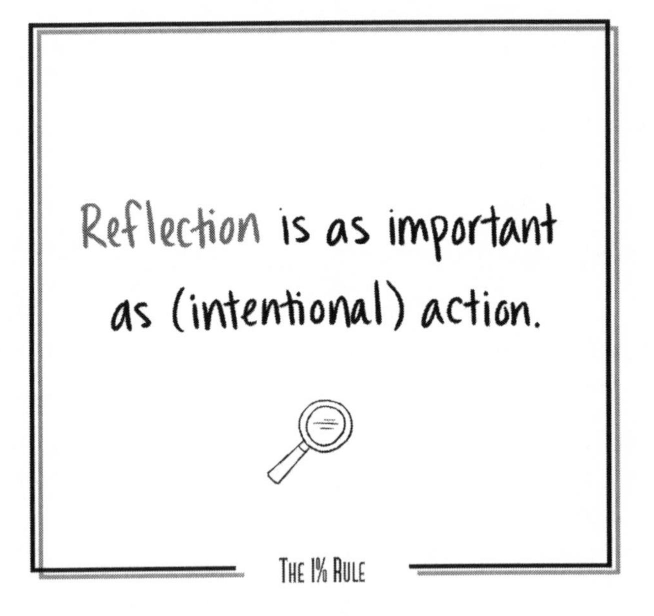

Note the key word in there: *intentional.* We've already covered that, but it bears a reminder. There's a world out there telling you to do more with very little intention or strategy. With this process, you will be pushing hard and taking daily steps. You'll be overcoming resistance, facing your fears, and moving the needle forward.

However, being refreshed and regenerated will give you the long-term stamina required to sustain the third pillar of endurance we covered earlier.

MYTH OF BALANCE

Balance is a myth and a sure way to let yourself off the hook. Sure, it sounds great in a corporate training binder, but it's not real life. Work and life balance assumes we can compartmentalize our lives, and they'll fit in perfect boxes—numbered, ordered, and in perfect alignment.

Furthermore, there's a veiled assumption that if we invest time and energy into business, it's going to come at the expense of another area of our lives.

This is not how it works, and thinking it is leads to massive amounts of frustration. Instead of attempting to balance your life, integrate it in a way where each part feeds the other. Allow your business and purpose to fuel your relationship, and find ways to integrate both. Allow your relationship to fuel your energy, vitality, and physicality—and integrate both.

This is how we raise all boats at once, making decisions designed to enhance and support all areas of life, not simply one or two.

Harvard Business Review's Stewart D. Friedman (Friedman 2014) says it best:

"[Balance] assumes we must always make trade-offs ... among the four main aspects of our lives: work or school, home or family (however you define that), community (friends, neighbors, religious or social groups), and self (mind, body, spirit). A more realistic and more gratifying goal is better integration between work and the rest of life."

STRATEGIC DISCONNECTS

If the concepts in this book have seemed intense so far, you're right: they are. In the last chapter on urgency and accountability, I referenced to a timeless text by Seneca, *On the Shortness of Life*.

If you read the text, you'll likely be woken up to the fact that our time here is short and will be over soon. Yet, within the urgency and intensity there also lies an important lesson of recharging, disconnecting, and allowing ourselves the space and time for restoration. The key here is to *intentionally* disconnect, instead of aimlessly succumbing to noise and distraction.

This is what I call strategic disconnects—being as intentional with your "off" time as your "on" time. In a nonstop world of stimulus, noise, and a cultural attitude of "sleep when you're dead" and "hustle harder," disconnecting may seem like a paradox.

Here's the deal, however: if you truly use the concepts and power of the 1% Rule, you're going to be using a high amount of mental and emotional bandwidth on a daily basis. Focus, productivity, and purpose are taxing, especially when we're used to short-term thrills and endless Facebook notifications.

If you're unable to balance this intensity with strategic periods of rest and restoration, you're going to burn out. Not a matter of *if*, but a matter of *when*. When you hit burnout, it's already too late, and many times you'll lose all the inspiration you had in the first place.

It's enough to make you give up on your dreams, so we must be careful. If we're here to endure and persist, we must place a high value on disconnecting. Below I'll detail the ways you can insert disconnection, and why they make you more creative, not less.

I'll also show you how you can apply these timely disconnects in a way that is simple and actionable.

TIMELY DISCONNECTS

Strategic disconnects in life fall into four main buckets:

Momentary. These last anywhere from fifteen seconds to a few minutes, and are designed to create interruptions and bookmarks throughout your day. For example, a walk around your office in the middle of the day can be a momentary disconnect. Closing your eyes and taking a few deep breaths before a big meeting is another. Setting an intention before you come home after a long day at work to see your family is an example of a momentary disconnect.

Daily. Daily disconnects are more expansive in time and include anything that takes from fifteen minutes to hours of disconnection and recharge. For example, establishing a 20-minute guitar habit is a creative disconnect. Meditation is a spiritual disconnect. Going on date night with your wife and kids is a relationship disconnect. Turning the laptop off and going on a hike is a physical disconnect. You get the drill.

Weekly. Weekly strategic disconnects set you up for

massive success, creativity, and new energy as you work through your endless tasks, projects, and responsibilities. These include longer disconnects such as date nights, trips, hikes, massages, retreats, a spa session—you name it.

Quarterly. These strategic disconnects happen four times a year and are designed to break from our environments and create a clean slate. Trips, experiences, retreats, adventures, and other forms of immersive events are some examples of a quarterly disconnect. Breaking the year into four quarters and creating a real demarcation line between one and the other will lead to massive clarity on your path.

Without a healthy dose of all these, it's easy to get stuck. There's an inherent power we've all experienced in breaking our patterns, even if we're executing and making progress. Sometimes, a simple shift leads to the breakthrough we've been looking for. We've all felt that place of intense work and burnout, fueled by caffeine. Sure, these intense sprints will happen, but if we don't create a strategic system to restore, we'll never have the physical, mental, and emotional capacity to see our visions come to life.

REALITY INTERRUPTS

Our environments can become our anchors for stagnation—or our catalysts for growth. In coaching hundreds of people virtually, I've found we are limited in the amount of transformation we're able to create, due to the inherent limitations of virtual training. Even though people can experience massive shifts through this training, there's one thing that stays the same on their path of growth: *environment.*

Our environment reminds us of who we've been and can induce the same state of mind we've had in the past. For example, when you step into your office environment, your subconscious is already lighting up parts of your brain associated with production, focus, social connection, and a typical work day. When you step back into your home life, your brain does the same in regard to family, relaxation, and connection.

There's a great benefit to this. It allows us to spend less energy consciously thinking about how to act in an environment. The downside, however, is clear: we can get stuck in our routines and patterns. When we're looking to create change in life, this can hold us back.

Dr. Joe Dispenza, New York Times Bestselling author, speaker, and Academy alumni, explains:

"To change is to become greater than your environment." (Dispenza 2017)

So how do we go about transcending our environment? Great question! This is where a powerful tool I call *reality interrupts* come to play. These are designed to shift your energy and get you primed for a new way of thinking, being, and doing. The power in reality interrupts is simple: we reframe our energy and create a powerful demarcation line and intention for what we're about to experience.

Interrupts help us clear space and let go of what's been, so we can create from a blank slate. These types of interrupts can be executed multiple times a day, as needed. Below, I'll describe each of the interrupts and how to put them into play in your daily life.

Physical Interrupt

The fastest way to change our emotional state is to change our physical state. The physical interrupt creates a powerful disruption in our lives designed to get us out of our heads and into our bodies. A physical interrupt can be anything from 25 push-ups to 10 burpees to a quick sprint—anything to get you breathing hard quickly. They usually last from 30 to 90 seconds.

**In the resources section, I provide several physical interrupts for you to use daily.*

Spiritual Interrupt

Spiritual interrupts create fantastic demarcations to the daily experiences we're all entering in and out of. They involve the practice of creating space and opening up opportunities to breathe, be creative, and achieve a new perspective. Take a moment to think about the last time you were running late to an important meeting. You hit red lights, you were tapping your foot, and were beyond anxious. This is not a place where you're open to new experiences or to connecting with people. A spiritual interrupt lasts 30 to 90 seconds and includes deep breathing, priming, and releasing.

**In the resources section, I provide several spiritual interrupts for you to use daily.*

Emotional Interrupt

Our emotions largely control our mindset throughout the day. If we're feeling sad and depressed, we're going to see the world as working against us. If we're excited and enthusiastic, challenges become opportunities and we experience life at a higher frequency. An emotional interrupt allows for a release of the emotions we've experienced. Research has proven that our emotions are stored in the body and build up over time if not released. But there are productive ways to release this repressed, unproductive energy. An emotional interrupt lasts 30 to 90 seconds and includes intense breathing, a primal scream, or closing your eyes and going deep into a place of gratitude.

**In the resources section, I provide several emotional interrupts for you to use daily.*

Mental Interrupt

With an average of over 60,000 daily thoughts, we've got a lot swirling around inside our heads. Add in the endless responsibilities, roles, tasks, and bills we need to deal with, and we can quickly feel overwhelmed. A mental interrupt allows us to let go of what's been and create space for what we're experiencing right here, right now. Mental interrupts include journaling, writing, reading, listening to empowering information, or even music for 30 to 90 seconds, to get ourselves in a new state of mind. They create a clear demarcation and bookmark between where we've been, and where we're headed.

**In the resources section, I provide several mental interrupts for you to use daily.*

These tools are designed to help you get focused, clear, and in the game. We've already established how much we struggle with daily clarity. These will help you on your path. At the end of the day, it's the simple habits we create and use daily that will have the biggest impact on our lives. We don't have to overcomplicate anything, as long as we're intentional.

SEASONS OF LIFE

With the 1% Rule, you'll be splitting up the year into four quarters. This will allow for maximum urgency, while keeping you focused on the next steps, ultimately leading up to 90 days of intentional work for both maximum fulfillment and incredible results.

However, we're also each on a personal evolution and operating under the seasons of life. Life is not linear, and different periods of your evolution will be dedicated to different seasons of life. The term *seasons* reminds us that we are constantly evolving, and it won't last forever.

While the concept of seasons comes from countless

ancient traditions, here I've simplified them to fit the context and practicality of our lives. They include:

Winter season

The season of winter in life is a time for taking inventory, reflection, regeneration, and rest. It involves downtime and recharging so we can set a new path. For many, it can be a tough season to stay in, especially for the hard chargers out there who are always looking to push harder. However, many of life's greatest insights occur during this season. It is a great time to set a path for new voyages.

Spring season

Spring season is about renewal and creation. During this season, you are blooming, creating, and producing. This is your time to take relentless action and execute. The conditions are ripe, and there is no time to lose. You've reflected and gone within all winter. Now use that energy wisely to execute at your highest potential. Right here, right now.

Summer season

Summer season takes spring's first step and kicks it into overdrive. If spring was launch, summer is growth and expansion at the highest level. This is where momentum and consistency start to kick in, and when incremental growth turns into exponential growth. There is no stopping you here. Ride the beautiful wave of momentum to shore and never look back.

Fall season

You've been working hard, creating, expanding, and growing, and now it's time to reap the rewards. During fall season, it's time to harvest the fruits of your labor. The early summer mornings are now over, and it's your time to celebrate before you enter another reflection period.

Why have I gone so deep into this concept? The reason is simple: it's important to understand that our paths of growth are not linear and even using a tool such as the 1% Rule will provide ebbs and flows of energy.

It's quite possible you will spend months or even a year in one of the seasons. The seasons are not meant to be taken literally, but rather conceptually. In creating this book, I'm knee-deep in the summer season of creation—launching two new programs, releasing an audiobook, creating a live event. However, it's winter where I live, and I know after a few months of this hard-charging energy, I'll spend some time reaping the rewards and reflecting.

CHAPTER 14
It's Your Time

Start. Through this book, we've gone on a journey together, and you're only getting started. It's your time—to create, to grow, and to expand. No more waiting, no more sitting on the sidelines, and no more analysis.

You know where you're headed in life, and now you have a strategic plan of attack. Using the 1% Rule, you can now take powerful dreams and ambitions and move forward every single day.

If you don't start now, this becomes *entertainment.* Or worse, it becomes another piece of material that sounded powerful, yet didn't turn into real-world results. Each time you create a new insight or gain an awareness of what's possible in your life and don't execute, you lose the life force within you required to truly believe.

Don't take it lightly. It's your time.

No matter where you're starting today and how disconnected you may feel from your vision, no matter what your general outlook on your life is, everything can change in the span of a few months.

GET IN THE ARENA

Whatever you do, get off the sidelines and into the arena. Put yourself in the game of life and watch how everything changes once you go from the stands into the game. Not only will your vision and possibility shift, you'll change the way you walk into a room, hold space in a conversation, and see the world. There is an unmistakable energy associated with living your path and dreams out loud in a world telling you what to do and how to do it.

It's *easy* to be a critic and to use your own inability to move the needle forward on your vision to attack others playing the game. However, time will pass and one day you'll wake up wondering why you spent your entire life watching someone else live out their dreams. Because no matter what happens on the field, they've won.

You won't learn invaluable skills when you're on the sidelines. You won't change your mindset. You won't sharpen your craft and your confidence watching others.

You won't create this inner belief of fortitude that only comes with self-reliance. You won't create your masterpiece if someone else is painting the brush strokes. Only you can, and there is no more waiting, there is no more time.

WASTED POTENTIAL

Take a moment and take yourself to the end of your life. We have no idea how or when it's going to happen, but we all know it will happen at some point. Imagine your last few breaths, surrounded by the people you love, the people you've created a life with.

Look around, and smile. As you do, ask a simple question:

Did I do everything I could in this experience of life, given all the gifts I've been blessed with?

This is not an answer you can fake in the moment, and you wouldn't want to anyway. Mortality cuts right to the truth, and you'll know how to answer. Sure, this is a little extreme and it's fabricated. But I'm often asked what drives me so much in life. People will ask me how I'm so ambitious and inspired, and I'll often reply:

How could you *not* be so driven and inspired? Don't you know that this experience is a gift?

As we mentioned earlier, your *why* must make you emotional and compel you to action. Personally, my *why* is deeply rooted in knowing time is finite, and I need to do everything I can to maximize the gifts I've been given. You too have been given countless gifts. No matter what your story is, what challenges you've faced, you're here, and you have a story to tell unlike any other.

It is a tragic thing to waste potential, and you and I have so much of it. It's within us, calling us to extract it and give it to the world, to serve ourselves through serving others. Don't waste your potential, because when you drop the narratives and stories you've been creating, you recognize the truth: you are so much more powerful than you give yourself credit for.

YOUR TIME IS NOW

I hope this is the last personal development and success book you ever read. Okay—*not really*. But I do hope you put it into action in such a way that you finally create the momentum you've been waiting for. I hope I meet you one day and you tell me about all the results you created. Not for my ego, but because you did the work. You realized your time is now and chose to stop waiting.

You don't have to wait for another New Year's or your next birthday to come around—it's time right now. Every moment you put off is another moment where the resistance wins and continues to pile up victories. Remember, the resistance wants to keep you small. The resistance wants to distract you from your dreams or tell you that you're not good enough. It wants to keep you chasing certifications in business to stop you from actually launching. It thrives on throwing you off course when you see your soul mate, and it tells you he or she is too busy in the coffee line. It loves when you click submit on a new program or course and then ask for a refund because it's not the perfect timing. Every time you let the resistance win, it comes at the expense of your self-trust. The great news is, your next opportunity to overcome the resistance is right now.

Even though it's technically never too late to get started, life gives us windows of opportunity. These windows are where magic is created, and the right conditions are thriving and ready. The seeds have been planted, the right amount of water and nutrients have been absorbed through the soil, and the sunlight has been bountiful.

In other words, it's time. The window of opportunity exists right now. If you wait, it may not be available to you any longer, at least not in the current capacity and format. Years ago, when I chose to extract myself from the East Coast environment and start a new life out West, I knew I only had a certain window of opportunity. If I didn't take the leap at that moment, I knew I'd be stuck forever.

I would have found an anchor to hold me there and would have rationalized why moving across the country and leaving everything I'd known in search of meaning wasn't a good idea. I would have given in to staying, and waiting, and then I never would have taken the leap.

SKYDIVING & DREAMS

Taking the leap is much like going skydiving—once you decide to go, you need to register as fast as possible. Because let's face it, jumping out of a perfectly good airplane is an idea we can easily talk ourselves out of.

We can blame the timing, our busy schedules, the insane level of fear. We can search Google for horror stories and accidents. We can say the weather isn't right, anything to keep us from taking the leap of faith. Every time I've jumped out of an airplane, I wanted to back out at the last moment, but I've pushed through the resistance.

Once you're climbing to 15,000 feet, there's nowhere to go. It's actually much less nerve-wracking at that point, because there are no other options available. It's you, the pilot, and the other jumpers, and there's only one way down: straight out and through.

There's no back.
There's no shortcut.
There's no turning back.

This level of trust required can be terrifying, yet exhilarating at the same time. The moment we let go and our hands come free and we realize we're dropping at 120 miles per hour, the world opens up.

It opens up because you made a bold decision in the moment and didn't let fear win. When you're bold, the world will respect you and open itself up to you.

But you've got to choose it—right here, right now.

NOTHING WILL CHANGE IF YOU DON'T

We've all met the person who talks a big game and tells us their world-changing intentions over and over. How they're going to quit their job and start their dream business, launch a six-figure sales funnel, and get in the best shape of their lives.

They'll give us a mouthful of their intentions and maybe even post on Facebook about their big plans. Strangers will compliment their discipline and drive, even though they haven't shown one ounce of either. Time will pass, seasons will change, and things are not only the same, they're further away from the goal.

Maybe this person is you. We've all been there. This common example outlines a simple, yet powerful reminder:

Nothing will change if you don't.

If you've been operating under the same exact inputs for years, it's fantasy to expect the outputs to magically change because you read a book or went through a seminar experience. Sure, you will achieve the insight and unlock the possibility within you, but it's not enough.

Nothing will change if you don't.

So, what will you change, starting right now? Do that.

YOU WON'T FIND YOUR SOUL MATE ON TINDER

You won't find your soulmate on Tinder.

You won't create a 6-figure funnel after reading Expert Secrets.

You won't be spiritually on fire after three meditation sessions.

You won't have a six pack after hiking your local mountain once.

Hate to break it to you, but this is real life. I can't tell you how many times someone has told me about their latest venture and how it's guaranteed to bring in $20,000 a month in passive income.

A few weeks later, I'll go to the site they created and it no longer exists. Their expectations were a level 10, yet they didn't have the courage to go through the ugly, intense, and sometimes excruciating process of creation.

Sure, there are unicorns in life, but I'm not putting my life on the line for a mystical creature — even a cute one. We're living in a world where we want the result without the process. The process is where the magic happens, where you stretch yourself, get uncomfortable, and—you know—experience life.

We're led to believe it will all be easy, but we're responsible for believing it. I'm all about dreaming big, creating powerful visions, unlocking the possibility—and then putting in the work.

The work isn't sexy, easy, or fun. These words are being written on a Saturday at 4:06 a.m. when it would be much easier to sleep. This is not easy right now—it's not supposed to be. My eyes are bleeding and I'd love to go to bed.

And what I keep noticing time and time again is people who want something but aren't willing to commit to the process.

(Hell, I've been there countless times.)

If you want to find a relationship that sets you on fire—**put in the work.**

If you want to create a thriving, profitable business—**put in the work.**

If you want to feel deeply connected—**put in the work.**

There's no way to slice it. Sure, you can speed up the process with deep levels of immersion, focus, and intensity, but there's still a process. The farmer doesn't plant the seeds and wake up the next day yelling in frustration because the tree hasn't bloomed. No, they understand the process, that with the right amount of sunshine, time, patience, and water, the tree will grow.

But you've got to want it and you've got to fall in love with the process more than the outcome. That's why you read this book. Now it's time for you to become these principles and be the beacon your social circle is looking for.

KNOWING WHAT TO DO

As you continue to live the principles we've showcased in this book, your vision and path will evolve. It's a beautiful, organic process that will stun you time and time again. Along your path, you're going to receive hints, messages, and opportunities you never had the perspective to see when you got started.

However, your vision and path won't scream at you—she'll *whisper.*

She'll say:

Hey, hey, slow down, and look over here. You'll be knee-deep in life, bills, responsibilities, and endless tasks. It's easy to ignore this call.

Then, a few weeks later, she'll whisper again:

I need you to look into this, over here. Once again, you'll stack logic and rationalization on top of this whisper once again, saying:

That doesn't make *sense.*

Time will pass, but she's feisty and persistent. Once again, you'll have an opportunity to listen and heed her call.

She's testing you, and asking:

Will he or she listen to me and take the first step on the journey into the unknown?

The first step may not look like any of the vision boards you've created.

It may look like needing to have a tough conversation.
It may look like needing to take a new route home from work.
It may look like saying yes to something you always say no to.

Yet the moment you make a new decision, she smiles and gives you a little more. She begins to trust you, and it becomes a beautiful partnership. Now that she trusts you, she gives you the big insights, because you've proven you will listen to her during the low-stakes situations.

And because you've put in the reps, you start to trust in the whispers that don't make any sense.

A whisper that you need to leave your environment and move cross country, now makes a lot of sense.

A whisper that the relationship you've been holding onto for dear life is actually the roadblock to your most powerful evolution.

A whisper that if you don't completely pivot in your

business right now, against all seemingly rational advice, you'll miss out.

Listening to her whispers is hard because she's not doing the work for you. She's guiding you into a path, and then it's up to you to put the puzzle pieces together.

Remember this, and cultivate the daily awareness and practice of tuning in to these messages. You already know what to do. Now, it's time to do it.

100 REASONS WHY YOU'RE WORTH IT.

As we finish our journey here on the 1% Rule, I want you to be inspired. Unlike the past, I don't want you to be inspired and excited about the outcome—not here. You're going to be inspired by the process, the resistance, the real, daily obstacles you and I will face at every level of our growth.

It's a different inspiration, one that is based on reality, not fantasy. Years ago, I sat in Dr. John Demartini's office for a consultation. I'd been frustrated with my fitness business and feeling a real lack of purpose and meaning behind it, even though it'd been my dream.

You've felt this too, when something fueled you for a certain amount of time but no longer fuels you today. I knew it wasn't simply the passing of time, but something gnawing and clawing at me for more.

That's when he gave me an assignment: write down 500 benefits of closing down, selling, or moving on from your fitness business.

"500!? That's impossible," I said.

"I'm waiting," he replied.

During the next hour, I almost broke my hand from the constant writing, but I identified 500 reasons. Once I got into the flow state of awareness, I couldn't stop writing. Ever since then, I've prescribed similar exercises to clients to get them clear, focused, and flexing the powerful muscle of deep noticing.

Today, you're off the hook. But we're going to identity 100 reasons why you're worth it. We're going to identify the reasons why your time is now, and there is no looking back.

- » You're right here, right now.
- » You're ready to create.
- » You have a powerful vision.

- » You've got gifts to share.
- » Your message is unique.
- » You're powerful beyond belief.
- » You're resilient.
- » You're open to learning.
- » You're here to grow and expand.
- » You know you've got a calling.
- » You know you're here to serve.
- » You know what to do at any moment.
- » You have immense self-trust.
- » You validate yourself from within.
- » You'll never quit, no matter what.
- » You know there is no growth in waiting.
- » You've shown yourself to be bold.
- » You honor and accept yourself fully.
- » You want it badly—for the right reasons.
- » You're a beacon here to guide.
- » You're reading this book.
- » You're ready.
- » You have your entire life experience.

- » You've developed yourself.
- » You'll never be more evolved than today.

AND SO IT BEGINS

And so it begins. It's your time to leave the safe harbors and set upon your voyage. There is nothing else you need. These concepts, stories, and lessons are yours. Make them your own.

It's been a riveting and humbling journey together, and I trust we will meet again out there on the seas of life. You deserve it. You know you are part of the 5% in the game of life who have the courage to listen to the voices of truth, instead of the ones of resistance.

Chart your path and fall in love with every part of your voyage: the anticipation, the first steps, the inevitable storms, the adversity, the growth, and the tears. Look at yourself in the mirror late at night and say:

I'm doing this.

That's what it's all about. So let's commit right here to live out loud, and take the first step today. Your beautiful journey awaits.

Onward.

NOTES, RESOURCES & MORE

We've taken a journey through the 1% Rule, and I'm honored to have you along for the ride. The 1% Rule was created through countless years of studying, interviewing greats, and teaching others to find the best of the best and discard what doesn't work.

In this section, you'll find notes and resources for each section, designed to take you to the next level. Every resource has been proven, tested, and qualified to ensure it's worth your time and energy.

RESOURCES

In this section, I'm including some of the best resources I've come across. Some were mentioned in the book, some weren't. I'll include a note and link or where to find them and why they matter.

Business

Resist Average Academy Podcast. Many references including interviews I've had on the podcast, and countless other episodes. You can find the Resist Average Academy podcast on iTunes, Sticher, Google Play and Spotify. Every week, two episodes are released – one interview style, one shorter version in a solo format.

Resist Average Tribe Experience. This virtual coaching experience is designed to help you bridge the gap from where you are today, to where you want to go, and is my most affordable program. Find out more at www.ResistAverageTribe.com.

The Pomodoro Technique, Francesco Cirilio. This technique was referenced several times in the text. https://cirillocompany.de/pages/pomodoro-technique

Pomodoro Online Timer. Online, free tool to track your Pomodoro's: http://www.marinaratimer.com/

RescueTime. A great tool to track your time spent online, free version works great. https://www.rescuetime.com/

Brain.Fm. Focused web-based app with research proven musical tracks designed to keep you on task. A favorite amongst entrepreneurs. http://brain.fm/

Dan Sullivan, Strategic Coach. One of the best in the game to shift your thinking from incremental growth to exponential. https://www.strategiccoach.com/

Storybrand One Liner Exercise. A tool I use on all my ventures and with most of my clients. https://www.youtube.com/watch?v=HFergI0UOAs

Health & Fitness

SEALFIT by Mark Divine. A great platform combining every aspect of life for training. https://sealfit.com/

Strava. My most used app for tracking endurance focused activity. https://www.strava.com/mobile

Spiritual Fitness Protocol. See below under strategic interrupts.

Spirituality & Meditation

Insight Timer App. One of the best in the business, amazing content and meditations. https://insighttimer.com/

Floating. Also known as sensory deprivation, search in your area and use this beautiful practice to deepen your meditation.

Chris Lee Meditation. Originally performed on the School of Greatness podcast with Lewis Howes. Starts at the 34:00 mark and a great way to cement your one-year vision, short and sweet: https://soundcloud.com/lewishowes/chris-lee

Dr. Joe Dispenza Meditations. Tested and proven by research, these meditations will deepen your practice. https://drjoedispenza-com.myshopify.com/collections/meditations-english

Relationships

5 Love Languages, Online Quiz. Designed to help you understand and communicate with your partner. http://www.5lovelanguages.com/profile/

The Way of the Superior Man, David Deida. A must

read for understanding the intricacies of polarity and masculine/feminine energy. https://www.amazon.com/Way-Superior-Man-Challenges-Anniversary/dp/1622038320

The Work, Byron Katie. A great tool to use with one's emotional challenges and judgement of self and others. http://thework.com/en

The 1% Rule Strategic Interrupts.

Physical

» Max push-ups or any other exercise for 60-90 seconds.

» Walk outside or around the block.

» 10 deep, full breaths with eyes closed.

» Primal yell. Find an open spot, ideally in nature where you can yell at the top of your longs.

» Shift and declare: 10 burpees, declare how you're feeling in the moment (i.e. "Angry! Inspired! Hungry! Focused!).

» Spiritual Fitness Protocol.

» Cold water therapy or contrast showers.

- Intermittent fasting, 16-hour fast, 24-hour fast or 3-day fast.

Spiritual fitness combines all of these and includes the following:

Step 1: Find a place where you can sprint.

Step 2: Identify a target to sprint towards.

Step 3: Three deep inhales and exhales, eyes closed and imagining your vision as the target.

Step 4: Open your eyes, and sprint towards your target at full capacity. See your vision coming closer and what it means to you.

Step 5: Achieve target, close your eyes and express gratitude and the feelings of achieving your vision.

Rinse and repeat for 4-6 rounds as needed.

Mental

- Listen to inspiring and empowering content for 5-10 minutes.
- Teach someone around you what you learned above, or something else you've learned recently.
- Sign up for a new class you've never done. Improv

classes, comedy, dancing, fighting, archery, guitar… choose one and go.

» Read 10 pages with your phone on airplane mode. Immerse yourself in the text.

» Notebook affirmation. Identify one affirmation, i.e. "I Am Greatness" and write it down to fill an entire page of one notebook.

Emotional

» Free flow writing. Set a 5-minute timer and write whatever comes to mind.

» Journaling. Re-affirm what you're feeling and put it down on paper.

» Byron Katie, The Work. Use the PDF referenced above and go through it.

» Identify your emotion, write down where it's coming from, close your eyes and sit with it for 3 minutes. No judgement, simply "what is." When you finish, declare the new emotion you're wanting to feel.

Spiritual

» 5-minute meditation, anywhere you are. Create space.

- Sensory deprivation / floating session, as mentioned above.
- Read 10 pages of a deep and explorative text.
- 10 deep, full breaths with eyes closed.
- Shamanic Breathing / Wim Hoff technique. Research these specific practices.

BIBLIOGRAPHY

Acuff, Jon. "The Art and Science of Finishing," November 5, 2017, *Resist Average Academy*, podcast, https://itunes.apple.com/us/podcast/ep-82-the-art-and-science-of-finishing-with-jon-acuff/id1073462154?i=1000394445955&mt=2

Amabile, Teresa and Steven J. Kramer. 2011. "The Power of Small Wins." *Harvard Business Review* 89, no. 5. https://hbr.org/2011/05/the-power-of-small-wins

Baker, Tommy. "The Integration Experience," August 10, 2017, *Resist Average Academy*, podcast, https://player.fm/series/resist-average-academy-knowledge-inspiration-action-motivation-business-growth-spirit-success-money-charisma-leadership/ep-72-the-integration-experience-with-tommy-baker

Beck, Martha. 2002. *Finding Your Own North Star: Claiming the Life You Were Meant to Live*. New York: Harmony.

Burchard, Brendon. 2017. *High Performance Habits*. Carlsbad: Hay House

Corpus Scriptorum Latinorum. 2017. "On The Shortness of Life." http://www.forumromanum.org/literature/seneca_younger/brev_e.html

Coyle, Daniel. 2009. *The Talent Code: Greatness Isn't Born. It's Grown. Here's How.* New York: Bantam.

Crawford, Robert. "Only Three Hours of Productivity a Day." Employee Benefits, November 22, 2013. https://www.employeebenefits.co.uk/issues/november-online-2013/only-three-hours-of-productivity-a-day/

Damon, Matt, interviewed by Sam Jones on *Off Camera with Sam Jones*, November 3, 2014. https://offcamera.com/issues/matt-damon/watch/#.WjfCl1Q-fBI

Dispenza, Joe. "Becoming Supernatural," December 11, 2017, *Resist Average Academy*, podcast, https://resistaverageacademy.com/86/

Duckworth, Angel. 2016. *Grit.* New York: Scribner.

Friedman, Stewart D. 2014. "Work + Home + Community + Self." *Harvard Business Review.* https://hbr.org/2014/09/work-home-community-self, December 2017

Gaijinass. "Who Is David Goggins?" Accessed on December 3, 2017 https://gaijinass.com/2012/11/24/david-goggins/

Godin, Seth. 2007. *The Dip: A Little Book That Teaches You When to Quit (and When to Stick)*. New York: Portfolio.

Grisham, John. 2017. "Do's and Don'ts for Writing Popular Fiction." *New York Times*, May 31, 2017. https://www.nytimes.com/2017/05/31/books/review/john-grishams-tips-how-to-write-fiction.html

Hardy, Darren. 2012. *The Compound Effect*. New York: Vanguard Press.

Jobs, Steve. Commencement Speech. Stanford News, June 14, 2005. https://news.stanford.edu/2005/06/14/jobs-061505/

Keller, Gary and Jay Papasan. 2013. *The One Thing: The Surprisingly Simple Truth Behind Extraordinary Results*. Austin: Bard Press.

Kotter, John. 2008. *A Sense of Urgency*. Brighton, MA: Harvard Business Press.

McRaven, William H. Commencement Address. UT News, May 16, 2014. https://news.utexas.edu/2014/05/16/mcraven-urges-graduates-to-find-courage-to-change-the-world

Millman, Dan. 2006. *Way of the Peaceful Warrior: A Book That Changes Lives*. Novato, CA: HJ Kramer.

Millman, Dan. "Living the Peaceful Warriors Way," January 30, 2017, *Resist Average Academy*, podcast, https://itunes.apple.com/us/podcast/ep-84-living-the-peaceful-warriors-way-with-dan-millman/id1073462154?i=1000395290434&mt=2

Morrissey, Rich.2009. "Michael Jordan offers scalding if not scolding comments at Hall induction." *Chicago Tribune*, September 12, 2009. http://articles.chicagotribune.com/2009-09-13/sports/0909120237_1_scalding-scolding-induction

Newport, Cal. 2016. *Deep Work: Rules for Focused Success in a Distracted World*. New York: Grand Central Publishing.

Olsen, Jeff and John David Mann. 2013. *The Slight Edge*. Austin, Texas: Greenleaf Book Group Press.

Parkinson, C. Northcote. "Parkinson's Law." *The Economist*, November, 1955. https://www.immagic.com/eLibrary/ARCHIVES/GENERAL/GENREF/P551100L.pdf

Pressfield, Steven. 2012. *The War of Art: Break through the Blocks and Win Your Inner Creative Battles*. Black Irish Entertainment.

Rowling, JK. "The Fringe Benefits of Failure, and the Importance of Imagination." June 2008, *Harvard Magazine*. https://harvardmagazine.com/2008/06/the-fringe-benefits-failure-the-importance-imagination

Ryniec, Tracey. "Applying Warren Buffett's Investing Lessons Today," Yahoo Finance, October 4, 2017, https://finance.yahoo.com/news/applying-warren-buffett-apos-investing-014001335.html

Schwartz, Barry. 2004. *The Paradox of Choice*. New York: Ecco.

State of Obesity, The. "Obesity Rates & Trends Overview," https://stateofobesity.org/obesity-rates-trends-overview/. Accessed November 24, 2017.

Vishwanathan, Sai Preethi, Levi Malott, Sriram Chellappan, and P. Murali Doraiswamy. 2013. "An empirical study on symptoms of heavier Internet usage among young adults." Advanced Networks and Telecommunications Systems (ANTS), 2013 IEEE International Conference, 15-18 Dec. 2013. DOI: 10.1109/ANTS.2013.6802883

White, Judith, Ellen Langer, Leeat Yariv, and John Welch. 2006. "Frequent Social Comparisons and Destructive Emotions and Behaviors: The Dark Side of Social Comparisons." *Journal of Adult Development*, 13, no. 1 (March). http://people.hss.caltech.edu/~lyariv/papers/DarkSide1.pdf

Want to Speed Up Your Integration of The 1% Rule In Your Life and Business?

FIND ALL THE RESOURCES, FREE WORKSHEETS, VIDEOS AND DONE-FOR-YOU TOOLS HERE:

www.1percentrulebook.com

SUPPORT THE 1% RULE TODAY

If the material in this book resonated with you, and you want to help support the mission and message, it would mean the world to me if you'd leave a review on Amazon. It takes one message, on one day, to change one life, and if a person who needs to hear this stumbles across it because of your help, that's amazing.

Simply scroll down to the book page on Amazon and click "Write a Customer Review." Each review is deeply appreciated and received with humble gratitude.

ABOUT THE AUTHOR

Tommy Baker is a writer, speaker, author, coach, and host of the Resist Average Academy, a top-rated iTunes podcast designed to give you the knowledge, inspiration, and action steps to live a life by design—never by default. Tommy's contagious enthusiasm and approach to life can be seen and felt in the wide array of content he creates, including podcasts, books, videos, and courses. As he likes to say, he doesn't have it all figured out—but he loves the process. Learn more at www.ResistAverageAcademy.com.

90142460R00178

Made in the USA
San Bernardino, CA
06 October 2018